The Commonsense Book
of Catholic Prayer
and Meditation

Hilda Graef

The
Commonsense Book
of
Catholic Prayer
and
Meditation

SOPHIA INSTITUTE PRESS®
Manchester, New Hampshire

The Commonsense Book of Catholic Prayer and Meditation is an abridged edition of *God in Our Daily Life* (Westminster, Maryland: The Newman Press, 1951) and contains minor editorial revisions to the original text.

Sophia Institute Press®
Box 5284, Manchester, NH 03108
1-800-888-9344
www.sophiainstitute.com

Nihil obstat: Edward A. Cerny, S.S., D.D., *Censor librorum*
Imprimatur: Francis P. Keough, D.D., Archbishop of Baltimore
July 24, 1951

Library of Congress Cataloging-in-Publication Data

Graef, Hilda C.
    The commonsense book of Catholic prayer and meditation /
      Hilda Graef.
      p. cm.
    Rev. ed. of: God in our daily life. 1951.
    Includes bibliographical references.
    ISBN 1-928832-51-2 (pbk. : alk. paper)
    1. Christian life — Catholic authors. I. Title: Commonsense book
      of Catholic prayer and meditation. II. Graef, Hilda C. God in our
      daily life. III. Title.
    BX2350.3 .G72 2002
    248.4'82—dc21   2002000075

02 03 04 05 06 07 10 9 8 7 6 5 4 3 2 1

Almighty, everlasting God,
who hast willed to restore all things
in Thy beloved Son,
the King of the whole creation,
mercifully grant that
all the communities of the nations
that are scattered by the wound of sin
may be subjected unto
His most sweet dominion.

Christ,
King of Kings,
have mercy on us.

Editor's note: The biblical quotations in the following pages are taken from the Douay-Rheims edition of the Old and New Testaments. Where applicable, quotations have been cross-referenced with the differing names and enumeration in the Revised Standard Version, using the following symbol: (RSV =).

Contents

Introduction

The Prioress of a contemplative convent was once heard at recreation to say of a prayerful young woman, "She lives in the world, *but* she has a spiritual life." Might we not say that this *but* sums up to perfection an attitude that has become all too common among religious and lay people in recent times? It is indeed quite in keeping with the modern trend toward specialization that the spiritual life, too, should have to be regarded more and more as a matter for specialists, for monks and nuns, whereas the average Catholic contents himself with fulfilling his "duties." This means that he goes to Sunday Mass, says his morning and evening prayers, but "humbly" (as he often expresses it) leaves greater ambitions to those who are called to a higher life. This, of course, is a wrong conception of the spiritual life. For what is this life? It is nothing else but the life of the spirit, the life of the soul. Every man has a soul; consequently, every man has a "life of the soul," just as every man has a life of the body.

We are all usually very careful about this life of the body: we feed this body three or four times a day; we protect it from cold and anything that might hurt it; and if something seems to be wrong with it, we go to the doctor for treatment. We certainly do not leave these things to specialists of the body — say, sportsmen or dancers — thinking that concern for wholesome food and similar things is only for them, but no business of ours. We do not expect to keep ourselves fit for our physical life on a cup of tea in the morning and a tomato at night.

Yet this is precisely what we do with our souls if we are content with a few carelessly said morning and evening prayers. On such a diet, the soul will do exactly the same as the body would in similar circumstances: it will shrink; and although, by the grace of God, it may not finally die by falling into mortal sin, it will at least be a case of "arrested development" — a dwarfed soul in a full-grown body.

For just as we have been given at birth a physical life to be tended and cared for, so we have received in Baptism a spiritual life, which must be nourished at least as carefully as the life of the body. How else can we expect to accomplish the will of God, which, according to St. Paul, is our sanctification?[1]

Sanctification is a big word. Are we really to aspire to that? After all, sanctity is a very rare thing, and we are perhaps inclined to relegate St. Paul's words to those "hard sayings" which, as far as we are concerned, are best left alone. With this decision we would do exactly the same as did the crowds who turned their backs on our Lord because "this saying is hard, and who can bear it?"[2] We must face it: what God wills for us is

[1] 1 Thess. 4:3.
[2] John 6:61 (RSV = John 6:60).

not an easygoing, lukewarm life; in fact, lukewarmness is just what He hates most, for we read in St. John, "Because thou art lukewarm and neither cold nor hot, I will begin to vomit thee out of my mouth."[3]

What He wills for us, then, is a life of sanctity. This great demand ought not to discourage us; on the contrary, it should fill us with confidence and boundless aspiration, for it is to be had for the asking. If we pray for other things — health, the removal of a particular temptation, success in our work — we must always make the condition: if it be Thy will. But St. Paul tells us explicitly that our sanctification *is* God's will, as does our Lord Himself when He bids us be perfect as our heavenly Father is perfect.[4] So we may ask for it boldly, persistently, without any fear that our prayer might perhaps not be pleasing to God. "Lord, please make me holy" is a prayer that is bound to be heard — if we really want it to be heard.

But there's the rub: he who wills an end must also will the means necessary to attain the end. If we ask God to give us holiness, we must also accept the means He chooses to make us holy. And this is where the difficulty begins, for sanctity will surely be given to us if we really desire it; but it is the work of a lifetime.

It is the work of a lifetime; and my life holds all the materials from which my sanctity must be fashioned; neither Carmelite cell nor bishop's palace is needed for it. A lawyer's office or a housewife's kitchen will offer us all the opportunities necessary

---

[3] Apoc. 3:16 (RSV = Rev. 3:16).
[4] Matt. 5:48.

for us to become saints if either of these, or anything else, is our vocation in life. For if we do not become holy, it will never be the fault of circumstances, which would really mean the fault of Divine Providence, which has placed us in these. It will be entirely our own fault.

This fault will have very serious consequences, and not only for ourselves. We complain that paganism is daily gaining ground, but are we doing anything to counteract it? For the paganism around us is our responsibility. The conversion of the world depends on us; we have our Lady's word for it, for she said at Fatima that if men devoted themselves earnestly to prayer and penance, Russia would be converted and the world would have peace.[5]

The more we deepen our spiritual life, the more shall we radiate Christ and give Him to others. We may not see anything of this influence ourselves; sometimes even all our efforts may seem useless to us, yet none of them will be lost. Did not God promise to save Sodom if He could find ten just men in it?[6] And do not all the lives of the saints bear testimony to the influence of even one really holy soul?

What our time needs more than anything else is not only contemplative convents, but also men and women living truly and deeply Christian lives in the world, in their homes, in offices, factories, schools, hospitals; who are spiritual oases, so to speak, in the desert of worldliness and godlessness around us.

[5] The Blessed Virgin Mary revealed this in 1917, when she appeared to three children in Fatima, Portugal.

[6] Gen. 18:32.

Sometimes people are afraid of embarking on such a life. They think that it means giving up all sorts of pleasures and luxuries. After all, it does mean living according to our Lord's words: taking up our cross, being poor, being ready for persecution, and similar things unpleasant to the senses. And they point to certain persons who sit in church all day and go about with long faces sermonizing in plaintive tone — no, surely the spiritual life is not for them.

It is unfortunately true that there is a type of "devout" person who frequents retreats and indulges in endless confessions and conversations with his much-tried parish priest or spiritual director. But such behavior is by no means a sign of a vigorous spiritual life. For to give ourselves to a truly spiritual life may mean some initial renunciation, but it brings with it such joy that those who lead it become a joy and comfort also to others. And how could it be otherwise, seeing that such a life brings us into ever closer contact with the Source of all joy?

The life of the spirit is a glorious thing that deepens and intensifies even earthly joys, the joys of family life, of friendship, of art, of nature. For it is the true life, the life for which man was created, which he enjoyed in Paradise, and which our Lord won back for him by the victory of the Cross. There are no repressions about it — unless we would contend that a gardener pruning a plant to make it bear more fruit "represses" its growth.

Having a spiritual life, then, is not an affair for the chosen few who enter convents, but the concern of every Christian; and it is the pressing need of the Church and of the world that as many Christians as possible should lead it. Of course, there are many problems and difficulties confronting the Christian who embarks on this task; a few of them will be discussed in the following chapters.

The Commonsense Book
of Catholic Prayer
and Meditation

Chapter One

≈

Base your faith on common sense, not on the miraculous

When a priest once recommended a young girl to the great St. Teresa[7] on account of her piety, St. Teresa was not impressed. "But has she sense?" she asked. For the nuns, she said, were quite capable of training her in piety, but good sense God alone could give. This may come as a shock to some readers; yet how profoundly true it is!

It is a very remarkable thing that so many pious people, who may possess a modicum of common sense in their ordinary life, seem to lose it completely as soon as they attempt to lead what is commonly called "the spiritual life." One of the worst evils due to a lack of sense in these matters is the desire for the miraculous, which shows itself in many ways.

There is, for example, the type of person who constantly arranges his or her life according to dates or according to "answers to prayer."

Let us make our meaning clear by a few examples.

---

[7] St. Teresa of Avila (1515-1582), Carmelite nun and mystic.

Somebody wants a job and makes a novena for the purpose. At the end of the novena, something entirely unsuitable is offered him. At any other time, he would have refused it at once, but it came on the last day of the novena; therefore, it must be the will of God, however unsuitable it may seem. Perhaps, he thinks, it is just God's way to make it appear so uncongenial at first, so that it may prove more wonderful afterward. It was offered on the last day of the novena, and, against all the rules of common sense, it is accepted and naturally turns out to be a disastrous failure.

Or someone has ardently been praying to St. Joseph for a house. On one of the saint's feasts, he happens to receive an offer from a real estate agent that he would have turned down on any other day, because the house is far too large and expensive, but the offer came on the feast of the saint; therefore, God must have had some mysterious plan with it. The offer is accepted, and the man is brought nearly to ruin.

What are we to say of such behavior? That people acting in this way have more faith than those who go by their reason? On the contrary. It is quite right to make novenas for a special purpose; it is right to ask the saints for their help; but it is wrong, and not faith but superstition, to base our decisions on what may be no more than coincidence. If we get such an "answer to prayer," let us first examine whether it really is one. If the job is suitable, if the house is what we need, we may well attribute the fulfillment of our desire to the intercession of the saint whom we have invoked. But our decision to accept the "answer" must be based on nothing else but the suitability of what is offered us. If we do not decide according to the laws of sound reason, and we find afterward that we have made a disastrous blunder, we must not attribute this to any fault on the part of God, but to our own inexcusable folly.

For God has given us our reason as our principal guide in the decisions we have to make. In fact, a disregard of our God-given reason in these matters is no less than an insult to the Second Person of the Blessed Trinity. "That was the true light," says St. John, "which enlighteneth every man that cometh into the world"[8] — words that are referred by theologians to the human reason, the image of the *Logos*, the Son of God, in which every man is created. Now, if we disregard our reason — this faint reflection of the Eternal Reason given us to govern our life — and instead rely on coincidences and self-invented signs, we insult our reason and, through it, the Divine Image in which it was created.

But, it may be objected, we read so often in the lives of saints of wonderful answers to prayer; how they asked and a sign was given them. Are not the saints our example? Why should we not follow them? Far be it from us to contend that we should not believe in wonderful answers to prayer.

All we would urge is not to take for an answer to prayer what is merely a coincidence. We do not think to misinterpret the Mystical Doctor of the Church if we apply to such asking for signs the words he wrote in regard to certain "ceremonious prayers." St. John of the Cross teaches, "What is . . . indeed intolerable is that certain persons desire to feel some effect in themselves, or to have their petitions fulfilled, or to know that

[8] John 1:9.

5

the purpose of these ceremonious prayers of theirs will be accomplished. This is nothing less than to tempt God and to offend Him greatly, so much so that He sometimes gives leave to the Devil to deceive them, making them feel and understand things that are far removed from the benefit of their soul, which they deserve because of the attachment which they have in their prayers, not desiring God's will to be done therein more than their own desires."[9]

Perhaps it may surprise those who are not very conversant with the saint's teaching that he not only condemns all superstitious practices, but also extols reason and places it as a judge above private revelation.

"For," he writes, "there is no necessity for any of these things (*viz.*, private revelations, etc.), since there is a natural reason and an evangelical doctrine and law which are quite sufficient for the soul's guidance. . . . [I]f certain things be told us supernaturally, whether we so desire or no, we must only receive that which is in clear conformity with reason and evangelical law. And then we must receive it, not *because it is revelation, but because it is reason,* setting aside all interest in revelation; and even then it is well to look at that reason and examine it very much more closely than if there had been no revelation concerning it. . . . Wherefore, in all our anxieties, trials, and difficulties, there remains to us no better and surer

---

[9]   St. John of the Cross (1542-1591; Carmelite mystic, and
      reformer of the Carmelite Order, known as the Mystical
      Doctor), *Complete Works*, "Ascent of Mount Carmel" (West-
      minster, Maryland: The Newman Bookshop, 1945), I,
      328.

means than prayer and hope that God will provide for us, by such means as He wills."[10]

This is a very important teaching, coming as it does from a Doctor of the Church, which gives us the principles by which to regulate our spiritual life. And the chief of these is to order this life by the light of our reason, to judge even private revelations — and, *a fortiori*, strange coincidences, "answers to prayer," dreams, and the like — by this light and by no other.

It is unfortunately true that many of us, when we embark on the spiritual life, imagine that by doing so we are entering a sphere in which the laws of ordinary human life are abrogated. We expect to live henceforth in an atmosphere of the miraculous, so to speak, where our prayers will be granted in wonderful ways, where we may even take liberties with God. Quite a few of us assume, misinterpreting the parable of the importunate friend,[11] that we can compel God by our prayers, as if He were bound to give us whatever we ask. Certainly we may ask God again and again for the things we need. But this is the condition: for the things we need in reality, not for those we think we need.

Now, what we really need, what we may ask for at any time, are the things that will ensure us the possession of God in eternity — that is to say, the virtues and the gifts of the Holy Spirit. This is the bread and the fish[12] that the Father will always give to our prayers. If we ask Him for humility or charity,

---

[10] Ibid., 165.
[11] Luke 11:5-8.
[12] Cf. Luke 11:11.

for fortitude or wisdom, He will always grant us an increase of these. But if we ask Him to make life easy for us, if we ask Him to remove the Cross and to grant all the many little desires that we have at this particular moment, it would be folly to expect Him to act in this way. He is indeed a Father, but not a weak, indulgent human parent who simply cannot refuse whatever his little boy or girl may choose to ask.

We sometimes hear people boast about how they are on familiar terms with God, going "straight" to our Lord, telling Him that He simply must get them out of this or that difficulty, that He cannot possibly "let them down" over such and such a thing.

Such a prayer is not Christian prayer, but comes perilously near to certain practices of idol-worshipers who threaten to maltreat their gods if these do not give them what they want. If we would but use our reason, it would tell us that God — being all-wise and all-powerful, as well as goodness itself — must necessarily know infinitely better than we ourselves what is to our profit and will give us the things we need most, although they may be, and often are, the very opposite of what we desire.

Unless we realize this with all clarity and accept unreservedly the consequences that follow from it — namely, that we may often receive those things we dread and be denied those we covet — we shall never be able to lead a sound spiritual life. For such a life, it is absolutely necessary to remove the craving for the "miraculous" and the extraordinary from the field of our spiritual consciousness and to pray with humility and sincerity the prayer of the agonized human nature of the Son of God: "Nevertheless, not my will but Thy will be done."[13]

We have neither in the New Testament nor in the Tradition of the Church any foundation for expecting that God will deal with us in some extraordinary way, solving our difficulties for us and dispensing us from using our common sense. The spiritual life is for the most part very humdrum. We practice the virtues even if we find them difficult; we pray even if we are in no mood for prayer; we put up patiently with tiresome work and uncongenial people; and we do all this for the love of God, even though we may not even feel this love in our emotions. From time to time, He will certainly give us rays of light and encouragement, but they will be the exception, not the rule. If a saint and mystic of the stature of a St. Bernard[14] exclaimed, "How rare the hour, and how quickly gone" when he was allowed to enjoy the presence of the Beloved, what can we expect, unfaithful and worldly as we so often are?

Does all this sound dreary, as if it were not worth the trouble? Certainly it is worth the trouble, all the trouble we can possibly take. It is worth the sacrifice of everything, even of our life. For we are here but as wanderers, having no abiding city. At the end of the journey, so often dreary, we shall have our reward, God Himself, the possession of the Father, the Son, and the Holy Spirit.

And according to the generosity of our surrender here will be our capacity of possessing God in all eternity. If we go to

[13] Cf. Luke 22:42.
[14] St. Bernard (1090-1153), abbot of Clairvaux and Doctor.

Heaven although we were lukewarm here, we shall certainly be filled with beatitude, but — to apply a spatial metaphor to what cannot, of course, be measured in terms of space — we shall be but small vessels, holding little of it; the intensity of our beatitude will be comparatively weak. But if we are truly generous, living here in the darkness of faith, because we love God and not our own little idiosyncrasies, He will enlarge our capacities in a wonderful manner, and we shall reap the fruits of our abnegation in life everlasting.

Let us, then, be sober, using the sense that God has given us, looking not for miracles but, rather, for opportunities to exercise our faith and trust. We may then probably have no wonderful stories to tell of all manner of marvels that have happened to us; but we shall live a sound spiritual life, firmly rooted in reason and in the faith of Holy Church.

Chapter Two

*

Be faithful to your everyday duties

As his rule and the orders of his superiors are to the religious, such are to the layman his duties of state. By these are meant his duties to his family, his obligations in his profession, in his circle of friends and acquaintances, and the like. And as the rule and the orders of his superiors take precedence over the personal inclinations of the religious, so do the duties of state over the wishes of the man and woman living in the world.

To give a concrete example: suppose a religious felt himself drawn to a more contemplative kind of life than is prescribed by the rule of his order, but was given no permission to devote more time to prayer than the half hour allowed. His plain duty, that which God evidently wills for him, would be to obey and sacrifice his inclination, however good and holy in itself. It is the same for people in the world: their everyday duties take precedence over even their most holy personal desires.

But here we are at once in the thick of one of the main difficulties of life in the world: who is to determine what exactly are a man's duties? For the religious, there is no problem: once his superior has spoken, he knows what God demands from him. But for the man or woman living in the world, things are far more complicated.

It is clear that the man who has to support a family has the duty to provide for their food and clothing and for the education of the children according to his social standing. Apart from this obvious obligation, there are others: he has to devote some time to his family, to their circle of friends; he will interest himself in the education of his children, in their amusements. Evidently all these things are willed by God and are very pleasing to Him, for they are a reflection in the creature of what the Divine Fatherhood means in the Creator.

The difficulty begins when the man feels that, in order to fulfill all these duties in a truly supernatural spirit, he must intensify his life of prayer, because otherwise there would be the danger of getting immersed both in work and in amusements in a completely natural way and so of endangering his very vocation as father of a family.

The same, of course, applies to the mother. She can surely, as St. Teresa says, find God among the pots and pans; but only if she also finds Him elsewhere; otherwise she becomes but a harassed housewife whose thoughts never leave the sphere of her domestic worries.

This is the danger on the one side. But there is danger on the other side, too. If the temptation to put work before worship is more pronounced in the case of men, the opposite is more specifically feminine. The man who is not punctual in his office because he has stayed too long in church is a rarer phenomenon than the woman who does not get the breakfast ready in time because she extended her thanksgiving unduly.

Be faithful to your everyday duties

There can often be a very real difficulty in how to reconcile the duties of our state with the requirements of our spiritual life, which, in its turn, is needed precisely in order to fulfill these same duties in the right spirit. And, alas, there is no superior to tell us what exactly is the will of God in this matter, how far the "duties of state" go in a particular case, and where they begin actually to encroach upon the legitimate needs of the spiritual life.

Nor can the confessor always give precise advice. Often decisions will have to be made on the spur of the moment. In other cases, it may be impossible to explain exactly all the circumstances; after all, we cannot keep a busy priest too long to advise on what are often questions that, with a little common sense and knowledge of principles, can be decided by ourselves.

We shall suggest in a later chapter how we can make time for God even in a busy life. Here we would only give a few considerations on how to resolve some problems that may occur every day.

We have said that it is the clear duty of the father to provide for his family according to his social standing. But in our society, where class distinctions are becoming increasingly obliterated, it is difficult to define "social standing." The husband of a wife with expensive tastes, the father of children who want schools and training courses that are really above his means may find himself in a dilemma: Is he justified in sacrificing all spiritual aspirations for the sake of money-making in order to be able to give his family what they want, or shall he draw a line and refuse what seems to him exorbitant?

Or take the case of a mother. She would like to spend a little more time in prayer, but there are her children wanting her to take them to dances and theaters and to provide meals for their friends. Is she justified in refusing sometimes and thereby risking that both husband and children may want to seek their recreation outside the home?

These are real problems; they cannot be brushed aside by the remark that in really devout Catholic families, such situations do not arise. For, alas, it is one thing to profess Catholic standards in words and quite another to put them into practice in daily life. The woman who wants fashionable dresses, jewelry, and furs may quite genuinely be convinced that it is only in the interest of her husband that she should not be put into the shade by his colleague's smart wife. His children may feel that they would not have a chance in life unless "the old man coughed up a little more" to let them go to an expensive college. Yet in such a case, it may be not only a "spiritual luxury" but dire necessity that the businessman, who lives in a world where everything is judged only by material standards, should have time for a minimum of prayer in order to save his soul. And more than that: if he contented himself with an adequate income and gave some time to spiritual pursuits, he might exercise a silent influence on his family that would cause them, too, to consider other than material advantages.

Of course, great tact is required in these delicate relationships. No service is rendered to religion by cramming it down other people's throats. The less obtrusive the religion of one member of the family is, the more good will it do to the others; a firm but tactful refusal to be turned into a money-making machine and a strong but silent spiritual life may have incalculable influence.

Such a strong influence will be exercised most often by the mother of the family. It is part of the vocation of the woman to sacrifice herself, and, if it is a question of the demands of her family and her own inclination for longer hours of prayer, the latter will usually have to be given up. It seems to us that this is as it should be. In our time of widespread disintegration of family life, no sacrifice a mother can make to preserve its integrity will be too costly. Her presence with her daughters at a dance, with her husband at a party, her participation in the amusements of her children and their friends will be more pleasing to our Lord than long hours of prayer; for these activities may well be the main cause, under God, that keeps her family out of many faults and leads them closer to Him.

Not every woman will achieve what Bl. Anna Maria Taigi[15] did; she gradually imbued her husband with her own distaste for worldly pleasures by making an exemplary home for him and their children. But in many cases, she will at least render these worldly pleasures innocuous. Fulfilling her duties as wife and mother to perfection will, for her, take the place of long prayers. (We naturally never mean to suggest that she should not have a minimum, nor that she should not give more time to prayer if she can do so without neglecting any of her other duties.) For God gives graces not only in prayer. If we are really

---

[15] Bl. Anna Maria Taigi (1769 - 1837), wife and mother who had the gift of prophecy and rose to great holiness through faithfulness to her humble, everyday duties.

wholly given to Him, He will give them whenever we need them — even when we are taking our family to the theater.

We have an excellent reason for this confidence. Did not our Lord perform His first miracle at a wedding? Our Lady, the perfect example of all mothers, had accepted an invitation to a wedding. She was there, not just looking on with some slight disgust for such worldly feasting, but concerned that the guests should enjoy themselves and that the host should not be embarrassed by the lack of wine. Her eyes were not turned up to Heaven, for this was not the right occasion for it, but down on the glasses of the party: "They have no wine."[16] The mother who prepares a feast for her children surely has a Mother in Heaven who will speak good things for her to her Son.

But the duties of state do not concern only the family. Since man's creation, they have also included the duty of work, for "the Lord God took man, and put him into the paradise of pleasure, to dress it and to keep it."[17] Alas, man being now a fallen creature, it is often difficult to harmonize our professional duties with the needs of the soul. It is true: the Mass is the center and mainspring of our life, and assistance at it, if regarded in the abstract, should take precedence over everything else. Yet if a doctor is called to a patient at six o'clock in the morning, he must go without his Mass and attend his patient.

Other situations may be less simple. Let us give an imaginary example to make our meaning clear. Take a lawyer whom

16 John 2:3.
17 Gen. 2:15.

someone wants to entrust with a difficult case, telling him, "You are the only person in whom I have sufficient confidence; my good name and my whole career depend on a successful defense." The case seems important, but the lawyer knows that if he takes it on, he will have to "write off" for many months all spiritual activities, from the daily Rosary to the Holy Hour on Thursday. On the other hand, if he brings it to a successful conclusion, it will mean an increase of fame and substantial gain.

Human life is full of such situations in which the motives become hopelessly entangled. In the present example, there would be the lawyer's genuine wish to help an innocent man to clear himself, but at the same time the pleasant feeling that he is regarded as the only person capable of giving this help, combined, moreover, with strong material attractions. What is he to do in a case like this?

It seems to us that here and in similar situations, where there is obviously a real danger to the spiritual life, we would have to examine very carefully whether we are really the only person capable of handling the matter. Such a consideration may lead to a very salutary humiliation for our own conceit and, in addition, might open our eyes to the merits of other people's work. For if there is someone else equally capable, there would be no reason why he should not be recommended. If, however, there were really no one else who could save the innocent man, then his defense would be an act of charity, and we could surely trust God to reward the sacrifice by an increase of grace.

For it has always been the principle of the saints to leave even the heights of contemplation when fraternal charity demanded it. The only question for us, who are not saints, and who therefore are generally not enlightened by the wisdom of the saints, which caused them to see things as God sees them, is to find out whether we really do things from the motive of charity or from love of our own importance, a desire to interfere in other people's affairs, and similar reasons.

For the beginners in the spiritual life, it is very hard, indeed, to find their way in this maze of mixed motives, but the more faithfully we use the means of sanctification that God has placed at our disposal, the more enlightened shall we become by this very wisdom of the saints, which makes them see things at a glance, without the long and painful deliberations that we have to make in the beginning.

Chapter Three

~

Make your work a means to holiness

One of the means of sanctification at the disposal of practically all men, except the sick and the infirm, is work. Ever since the Fall of man, work has borne a double aspect: it is a fulfillment of human possibilities, and at the same time it is a chastisement of human sin.

In the second chapter of Genesis, we are told that "the Lord God took man, and put him into the paradise of pleasure, to dress it, and to keep it."[18] As God had "worked" six days in creating the world, so man, made in His image, was also to work in the world in which God had placed him. This work in Paradise, then, must have been a work resembling the "work" of God; that is to say, it must have been creative (in the human sense) work that developed all the faculties with which human nature had been endowed, both physical and intellectual abilities. For Adam was called not only to tend the Garden of Eden, but also to give names to all living creatures[19] and

---

[18] Gen. 2:15.
[19] Gen. 2:19 ff.

thus, by naming them, to recreate them in some way, to assimilate them intellectually.

Two conclusions may be drawn from this work of Adam in Paradise. First, work must be necessary for man, or God would not have imposed it on him immediately after his creation; it must be an essential ingredient of human life. Second, work must be perfectly compatible with even the highest forms of contemplation, for Adam in Paradise was in constant intimate relationship with God, and contemplation is precisely this.

But when sin came into the world, work, too, took on a different aspect. Then God said to Adam, "Cursed is the earth in thy work; with labor and toil shalt thou eat thereof all the days of thy life. Thorns and thistles shall it bring forth to thee; and thou shalt eat the herbs of the earth. In the sweat of thy face shalt thou eat bread till thou return to the earth, out of which thou wast taken."[20]

What had been a fulfillment of the human being now became punishment. But, by the mercy of God, it was not only a punishment; it also became a means of making reparation for sin. After the Fall, then, work was no longer only a reflection of the divine creative work, although this aspect was never entirely lost. It was also penance, drudgery, painful labor. Only rarely are these two aspects of work completely separated from each other.

Even the creative and satisfying work of the artist, the scholar, and the gardener will normally contain elements of drudgery and boredom. The resistance and imperfections of

---

[20] Gen. 3:17-19.

the material with which we have to work, our own inability to express perfectly the idea that is in our mind, all manner of circumstances not immediately connected with our work, such as excessive heat or cold, physical indisposition: all these will bring the element of penance even into work that would, in itself, be perfectly satisfying.

Nor is the work that is generally considered sheer drudgery entirely without its redeeming features. The mere knowledge of having accomplished the day's task to the best of our ability brings a certain satisfaction. Even the most boring and inhuman work — having to turn the same handle hour by hour, typing one address after another all day long — has this element of having done what we have been given to do — work that, after all, it was necessary to do for the good of the whole, whether factory, business, or any other establishment.

Yet, if work is to become a means of sanctification, it is not enough to regard it merely from this natural standpoint; it must be taken up, integrated into the supernatural sphere. The first condition for this is that our work should be done deliberately for God — which, of course, rules out *a priori* all work that would involve sin, such as, say, working in a gambling house or a contraceptive factory. Even if it meant a lack of work or the loss of unemployment compensation for refusing to accept such a job, we would have to endure that, just as the first Christians could not be soldiers or civil servants because it involved sacrificing to the gods, and as English Catholics after the Reformation were debarred from most professions on account of the oath of supremacy. But apart from such exceptional circumstances, all work can, and should, be done for the glory of God.

But this first intention of doing our work for God is not enough; it will have to be not only frequently renewed but also purified. For in every type of work, there will be many difficulties and temptations, and unless we can overcome these, our work will lose much or even all of its sanctifying power. Here we can do no more than give a few examples of some of the dangers with which we are faced.

We will first consider what we may conveniently call the "creative" and "intellectual" type of work — the two terms used in a complementary, not in a synonymous, sense; for there are many intellectual professions that are not creative, and vice versa. Now, one of the principal dangers of this type of work is that we grow so engrossed in it that it becomes an end in itself; that prayer, our duties to our family and friends, all else, in fact, is allowed to go by the board because we must get on with our work. We all know the artist or the author, the scholar or the industrialist who is so taken up with his new picture or book or business scheme that no one dares come near him for fear of interrupting the great work. This attitude will cause a man no longer to work for God but to put his work in God's place by making a fetish of it. This is what so often makes scholars, businessmen, politicians, and others somewhat inhuman; their work is no longer a means of sanctification but an end in itself.

There is another danger that is frequently connected with it; it is to make our work a means of self-aggrandizement. "This is my picture, my book, my business: I am the creator." It is very natural, a very human temptation. Yet, if we give way to it, our work will become a snare to us rather than a means of sanctification, because it will pander to our instincts of self-assertion and spiritual avarice, however generous we may be in material things.

It is essential that we should realize these temptations, for this is the first step to overcoming them. The second step is to take the necessary practical precautions; for example, to assign a certain amount of time to other pursuits, to spiritual duties, to our family and friends, to books on other than work-related subjects, so as to prevent ourselves from being eaten up by our work. If to this we add assiduous prayer against these special temptations, it is quite probable that it will be heard in a manner we had not anticipated: we may be given the divine answer in the form of setbacks, failures, criticisms, or illnesses that we may find very hard to bear, but which are wonderful means to purify our motives and to make our work more and more truly a means of sanctification.

If becoming too absorbed in our daily tasks is the temptation of the fortunate ones whose work is creative or intellectual, the difficulties of the many whose job is sheer drudgery are far different. Naturally, it is not within the scope of this book or within the competence of its author to deal with this, but we cannot bypass the question of how the Christian worker might integrate his inhuman and mechanical work into his spiritual life. There really seems no other way but to regard it as a penance — as a penance, however, not only in a negative but also in a positive sense.

The saints have always undertaken voluntary penances for the conversion of others. Can we doubt that a worker who fully accepts and offers to God for his fellows all the tediousness and boredom of his work will reap rich rewards in the efficacy of his apostolate? It is perhaps one of the hardest penances imaginable for a Christian to be tied to a soulless job, never seeing the finished product of his labors, or, if he sees it, probably not being able to love it because it, too, is a soulless, ugly, machine-made thing. But it is the most generous and, hence, the most efficacious thing to accept precisely this as the cross that Christ has told us to take up in order to follow Him.

Besides, if all truly Christian workers left their factories, the last chance of Christianizing workers in the factories would be gone. No, better far to accept the conditions in which Divine Providence has placed them (or are we to suppose that factories are outside the scope of God's Providence?) and, by filling them with the supernatural spirit of penance and vicarious suffering, transform them into sources of grace for ourselves and others.

But to be able to do that, we have to build up resources of spiritual strength. And it seems that it is one of the graces given to the modern worker that he has a comparatively large amount of free time, which, if used in the right way, would enable him to build up these resources, so that, despite the unsatisfactory nature of his work, his whole life would rest on solid foundations.

Chapter Four

⌒

Grow holier even through recreation

Many people find it difficult to "supernaturalize" their spare time. Without their meaning it to be so, it somehow gets taken up with a hundred and one little jobs and distractions, so they can truly say that they "haven't a minute to themselves." And often, paradoxically, the more time they have free from work, the less time they have. The truth is that they just fritter away their days nobody knows how and, consequently, are in a state of perpetual agitation with a "nervous breakdown" at the end.

But when God had created man, He ordained that for six days he should work and on the seventh day he should rest. We shall later deal with the need for recollection, which evidently has to be practiced in our spare time. Here we would only stress the need for relaxation, so essential for every balanced life. Unless the natural life is balanced, the spiritual life cannot be healthy; for grace does not supplant nature but perfects it.[21]

---

[21] Cf. St. Thomas Aquinas (c. 1225-1274; Dominican philosopher and theologian), *Summa Theologica*, I, Q. 62, art. 5.

Therefore the alternating rhythm of work and rest is a divinely ordained law of our life, affecting both body and soul. For if we live in a perpetual rush, incapable of taking a proper rest from time to time, our spiritual life will show the same signs of lack of balance as our natural life: we shall be restless, trying now one devotion, now another, changing confessors and methods of prayer, and eventually we shall end up in a state of utter confusion and exhaustion. No, we must know how to work, but we must also know how to "play."

What is perhaps the greatest need of us modern city dwellers is to regain contact with the nature that God has made. A walk in the country, in the woods, or through the fields will almost imperceptibly bring us nearer to Him who created them — a leisurely, relaxing, almost "contemplative" walk; we are thinking of St. John of the Cross, taking his friars for walks in the country to make them relax in the presence of God. For our modern habit of rushing through nature in cars or, a little less unnatural, even on bicycles, deprives us of the very real, strength-giving contact with the earth, deprives us also of discovering solitary, hidden little paths where all the rush, the haste of our lives can fall off. God walking in Paradise, in the cool of evening will, perhaps, also walk with us on such a peaceful, leisurely walk.

The saints knew how to relax. Think of St. Teresa playing the tambourine at recreation. It was she who said, "God deliver me from frowning saints."[22]

---

[22] St. Teresa of Avila, *Complete Works* (London: Sheed and Ward, 1946), III, 351.

Grow holier even through recreation

Very often our recreation will take the form of being together with our family and friends. The joy of being able to talk and play unrestrainedly without having to watch our words or to keep up appearances is in itself a recreation of our being and at the same time a powerful means of sanctification. When we say "without having to watch our words," we do not mean by this that we are allowed on these occasions to speak uncharitably or unkindly about others. On the contrary, although we may be "off duty" in every other respect, we are never so as regards the two great commandments. If we use these gatherings to preserve and strengthen fraternal charity, they will become for us and for others powerful sources of sanctity as well as of joy.

For Christianity is a religion of joy. The Church herself teaches us to rejoice. The *Alleluia* never leaves her lips except in the time of fasting and sorrow before the overwhelming happiness of Easter. The Church is not, as outsiders often assume, a tight-lipped spinster, grudging men every little bit of happiness. She is a loving Mother who wants to see her children rejoicing. Surely it is not by chance that our Lord allowed Himself to be seen at weddings and suppers, even to risking to hear Himself called "a glutton and a wine drinker,"[23] or that marriage feasts play so important a part in His parables, and that He spoke of Himself as the "Bridegroom." For Christianity is the religion of the whole human life — which is made up of joys and sorrows, of birth and death, of the Star of Bethlehem and the Cross of Calvary. "Whether you eat or drink, or

[23] Matt. 11:19.

27

whatsoever else you do, do all to the glory of God," says St. Paul.[24] The only condition is that our joys, our festivals, and our holidays should be such that our Lord may share in them.

Why should we not go and see a play or a good film? Aristotle spoke about the *katharsis*, the purification of the emotions that should be brought about by every drama. It is one of the highest gifts of men, one of those that reflect the Creator very clearly, that they can invent or describe human characters and situations that affect us almost as powerfully as reality itself, although we know all the time that they are not real. To forget for a little time, while we see a play or read a novel, our own circumstances and worries and to be absorbed in those of others can be very salutary, for it may give us back a sense of proportion that we lose so easily if we are taken up completely in the daily round of duties and cares.

Of course, these forms of recreation must be well chosen. Far be it from us to advocate only "instructive" or "religious" plays and films. But in order for us to enjoy them "with our Lord," as it were, they must possess certain moral and artistic standards without which they simply could not be considered entertainment fit for Christians. Films, plays, and novels in which crime, adultery, or even only wholly material pleasures are glorified, which only play up to the worst instincts of man, are not compatible with the desire to lead a truly Christian life. Our good sense will usually tell us where to draw the line in these matters, and the line will have to be drawn even if some of our pagan friends should consider us narrowminded and scoff at us.

[24] 1 Cor. 10:31.

Grow holier even through recreation

In former times, when film, TV, and radio had not yet penetrated into the most remote villages, amateur theater, concerts, and the like were favorite forms of recreation with many people. Although they may often not have come up to high standards of execution, yet it seems to us a great pity that they should have fallen into desuetude almost completely. For just because our civilization has become so entirely mechanized, an outlet for man's creative instincts is the more necessary where it is still possible, and that is precisely in his recreation.

A person who relies for his very recreation entirely on the ready-made entertainments provided by the various industries must necessarily become warped — even in his spiritual life, which will probably take the same line and become just a mechanical recitation of ready-made prayers, without a thought or aspiration that comes from his own heart. Mental and spiritual laziness is the death of the soul; the torpor of the mechanized mind is not a favorable material for grace to work on. King David danced before the ark;[25] St. Teresa took her tambourine and did the same; St. Catherine of Siena[26] loved to sing. We also should sometimes use our God-given talents, however small, to recreate ourselves, and not always rely on music and pictures "out of the tin."

Of course, we are active ourselves when we play tennis or football. But there is a difference between modern sports and the partly physical recreations of the saints: theirs were only partly physical, being the bodily expression of the joy of the

[25] 2 Kings 6:14 (RSV = 2 Sam. 6:14).

[26] St. Catherine of Siena (1347-1380), Dominican tertiary.

soul; whereas recreation by football, etc., is wholly physical, the exuberance of the body only, not of the soul also, that finds its outlet. Therefore, although a perfectly legitimate and desirable Christian recreation, sports alone are not enough. The man who leads a genuine spiritual life will probably instinctively go to other recreations that provide relaxation for the soul as well as for the body.

Chapter Five

⌒

Learn to benefit from your sufferings

Suffering, in one form or another, is part of every human life. But for the Christian life it has a special significance. The God of Christians died on the Cross, and, as He Himself said, the disciple is not above his Master and has to expect and accept suffering and persecution when and as it comes. Really, suffering can be understood only in terms of the Cross; else it would be meaningless — due to the caprices of some malign power, the jealousy of the gods, as the pagans tried to explain it.

But in Christianity, suffering has a double aspect: on one hand, it is punishment and satisfaction for our own sins and, on the other, a means of obtaining grace for our neighbor and for the Church. As such, it has always been regarded and even sought by the saints: "To die or to suffer," said St. Teresa; and St. Catherine of Siena desired suffering in order to ward off the calamities threatening Rome because of the sins of her age.

Should we, then, ask for sufferings? As we have seen, the saints have done so from time to time. We also read quite often in the lives of devout people that they asked for suffering for a certain purpose. And immediately some strange illness befell them; they became lame or blind or were stricken with some other such malady. And after some time, when the purpose of this vicarious suffering was said to have been achieved, they became as suddenly well again. This kind of thing happened quite frequently in their lives. Should we do the same, therefore, and pray to be given suffering?

It seems to us that the answer must be no. We find no evidence in the Scriptures that suffering should be sought. Our Lord Himself teaches us in His prayer to say to our Father: "Give us this day our daily bread" and "Lead us not into temptation." And His own prayer before His Passion was "Not as I will, but as Thou wilt."[27] He did not teach us to ask for suffering; but He did teach us to accept it generously when it comes. In fact, two of the eight Beatitudes are reserved for those who suffer: "Blessed are they that mourn, for they shall be comforted" and "Blessed are they that suffer persecution for justice' sake, for theirs is the kingdom of Heaven."[28]

In these words of our Blessed Lord, the Christian attitude toward suffering is summed up: it is to be one of loving acceptance. But we are not told to provoke it or to pray for it. Still, if this is so, how are we to regard the practice of the saints and other holy people that we have mentioned above?

Let us first be quite clear about one thing: suffering in itself is not a good. It is a defect; it is a consequence of sin. If man had not fallen, he would not have known suffering, as little as the blessed angels know suffering. There is no suffering in God;

[27] Matt. 26:39.
[28] Matt. 5:5, 10.

when He desired to make atonement for human sin by suffering, He had to take to Himself a human nature, so that suffering might become possible to Him in this nature united with the Divine Word, who, in Himself, is impassible.[29]

Suffering, then, is not to be desired for its own sake; and, indeed, only perverted creatures can so desire it. It is one of the absurdities of some modern non-Catholics to assume that Catholic saints desire suffering because they get some unhealthy thrill from it. Nothing could be further from the truth. The saints, with their ordinary human feelings, hate suffering as much as anyone else; but because they love Christ more than themselves, they desire suffering in order to become more like Him and to share in His work of Redemption — filling up in their body, as St. Paul says, what is lacking in the sufferings of Christ.[30] Hence, their desire for suffering has a purely supernatural motive.

Now, the saints are given to us for our example; and yet we have answered no to the question of whether we should pray for suffering. Not all that the saints have done can serve as an example to be imitated by everyone. We cannot all enter convents or preach crusades or look after lepers, although all these activities are excellent and very pleasing to God in themselves. And just as they require a very special call from God, so does the vocation to suffering. If we have a family to support, we would displease God greatly if we suddenly asked to be stricken with a terrible disease. But even if we are alone in the

[29] That is, beyond the reach of suffering or harm.
[30] Col. 1:24.

world, we do not think that prayer for great suffering would be pleasing to God without a very definite call. For one thing, it would imply a good deal of presumption. For to bear suffering — even comparatively small suffering — patiently and serenely requires a high degree of Christian perfection, and who are we to presume that we have reached such a stage?

In the case of the saints, these two factors were always present: their prayer for suffering was made in response to a special vocation and at a time when their union with God had reached a high degree. As to those stories of devout persons asking frequently for suffering and always obtaining exactly what they want, we think it advisable to receive them with great caution. More often than not, these sufferings are of a hysterical nature; they appear and disappear suddenly; and the charity and patience of these self-styled "victims" in other matters often leave much to be desired.

Let us make no mistake: God is not pleased with wonderful daydreams: how much we would suffer for Him, how patiently we would endure everything, if He would only send us something really great and glorious. If we pray for such things, our prayer may often be heard, although in a very unexpected manner. Here I am, dreaming of how marvelous it would be to be stricken with a very painful illness and, lying crippled on my bed, greeting the doctors, the nurses, and all my friends with a heavenly smile that would show them how deeply united I am to God and would bring them all closer to Him. So, "Please, Lord, send me suffering, that I may further Your kingdom by it." Next morning I get the answer. The bacon comes up rather cold and tough. I rage interiorly, being prevented from making a scene only by the thought that the maid might give notice. Next thing, of course, I miss the bus and consequently push an old lady aside in order to get the next one. And, finally, to fill up the cup, my secretary has called the office to say that she is sick with flu and cannot come in. And here I am, with double the day's work on my hands; and my temper is such that no one dares come near me for the next twenty-four hours.

Well, is not this an answer to prayer? "You silly child," the Lord seems to say, "here you are dreaming about your heroic patience in terrible sufferings — and now you cannot even muster sufficient patience to endure a few tiny pinpricks with equanimity. Learn first to bear the ordinary little trials of everyday life for love of me, and then you may perhaps be given something greater to endure."

This happens often, does it not? And of course, in a way, it's just these pinpricks that are so hard to bear — and so salutary! For there is practically no danger of pride in these small victories over self, as St. Thérèse of Lisieux[31] knew so well. On the contrary. If I do not fly into a temper because the breakfast tea is cold or because I have missed the bus — well, that is really nothing to be proud of; everybody can have a sufficient grip on himself not to give way to outbursts of temper over such trifles. Nevertheless, it is just these pinpricks that are sent by God every day, and, if borne for love of Him, they may in the end make real saints of us.

[31] St. Thérèse of Lisieux (1873-1897), Carmelite nun and Doctor.

However, although we are not to seek suffering presumptuously, we should accept it resignedly, if not joyfully, when it comes. Very often God sends us precisely the suffering that hurts us most. Why just this? Why take from me this beloved person? Why send me ill health at this particular moment, when I have already so many other difficulties? Why? The reason is known to God alone; although quite often, years later, we begin to see what was the purpose of this particular suffering at this particular time.

While it lasts, however, the suffering often appears quite purposeless. How pointless and absurd did it seem to Peter that our Lord should suffer — just when He seemed, in the opinion of His disciples, at the beginning of a glorious career as the Messianic King of Israel. In the whole history of mankind, there has never been anything more patently absurd than the sudden ignominious end of a great preacher and wonder-worker who, although He had raised others from death, seemed unable to avoid death Himself. Yet this death defeated death and gave the whole history of mankind its meaning.

At the same time, it gives meaning to all individual suffering. Ever since St. Paul wrote to the Colossians: "I rejoice in my sufferings for you and fill up those things that are wanting of the sufferings of Christ in my flesh, for His body, which is the Church,"[32] Christians have regarded suffering as the most efficacious means of cooperating in the redemptive work of Christ. Therefore, when suffering is sent to us, we should receive it as a gift from God, lovingly, gratefully. For, as we have

[32] Col. 1:24.

said before, suffering is not something good in itself; its efficacy depends on the use we make of it. If we receive it grudgingly, complaining all the time and asking why just we should have to endure so painful a trial, it will be of no value at all; it may even make us bitter and therefore displeasing to God.

We hear it said sometimes by pious souls in regard to people who have suffered much, although with a bad grace, "Oh, he will not have a long Purgatory. Think how much he has had to suffer." Although such a remark is kind, it is not true — else even great sinners, provided they had had much suffering in their lives, would go straight to Heaven. Suffering is only the raw material of sanctity, so to speak; but, if used in the right spirit, it is wonderfully efficacious.

What, then, is the "right spirit"? Surely the spirit in which our Blessed Lord accepted His Passion. Here, we think, the Agony in the Garden is of the deepest significance. For it shows us that our Lord was truly human and had humbled Himself even unto the natural fear of death that every human body feels. His whole physical nature revolted from death — and more strongly, because it was so perfect and so intimately united to the immortal Divinity. But His will, in perfect obedience to the Father, overcame this natural fear: "Not as I will, but as Thou wilt."

How much courage should that sublime scene in the Garden give us! Whenever we are in fear, whenever our poor human nature writhes in agony, there is our Lord, to whom we can turn with the certitude of finding perfect understanding and help. Let us just take one or two instances of the most ordinary forms of suffering.

We are hospitalized and in pain. How often, instead of making the most of this silent form of the apostolate, do we miss our opportunities? We are cross with the nurses, who can never do anything right and whom we cause no end of trouble by our constant grievances. When our friends come to visit us, instead of allowing them to distract us a little, we recount with relish the detailed history of our illness with all its symptoms, incidents, views of the doctors (generally wrong) and our own (always right). Of course, this kind of behavior is very human and understandable, for when the poor body is tormented by illness, the mind and will have a far harder task to assert themselves. Yet we should try as much as possible to overcome this weakness; if we do, the more easily shall we bear our pains.

For some patients, the nurses seem always to have time, and their bedside is never without friends or relatives during visiting hours. Why is this? They always have a grateful smile for those who look after them, and their friends, far from having to listen to tedious accounts of their case history, always find a ready ear for their own troubles. They are not greeted with reproaches for not coming more often; for the patient knows that, while he is in the hospital, the world outside goes on as usual, the office work must be done, conferences have to be attended, or the husband's dinner has to be cooked, and the sick visit has, more often than not, to be fitted with great difficulty into a crowded day. If our friends bring us flowers or other presents, we should receive them with appreciation and gratitude, even if they are not exactly what we want at the moment.

And if the illness should bring us even to the threshold of death? Shall we not then be released from all concern for others? Our Lord, in the excruciating torments of death by crucifixion, was not concerned with His own but with the fate of His enemies, whom He forgave; with the good thief, to whom He promised Paradise; with His Mother, whom He entrusted to the care of St. John. And only at the supreme moment — and that, probably, for our consolation rather than for His own belief — did He allow Himself to cry, "My God, my God, why hast Thou forsaken me?"[33]

Perhaps we may say that this is all very well. Yet how can we presume to follow such an exalted example as that of our Lord, the Word made flesh? The saints have thought otherwise.

And if our Lord seems to be too high above us for our imitation (a mistaken view, since He proposed Himself to us as our model from which we should learn), surely a little French bourgeois girl will not be too difficult to follow. St. Thérèse of Lisieux, in her long-drawn-out agony, suffered tortures of pain, but she never lost her smile and concern for others, for all was offered to our Lord in a holocaust of love. If she could do it, why not we?

Of course, not from our own strength. But surely, if we ask our Lord persistently and earnestly to give us grace to suffer as He would have us suffer, He will not refuse our prayer. With His assistance, we can even face death with courage, for it is but the door that, while shutting upon the world, opens into Heaven.

[33] Matt. 27:46.

But physical suffering is not the only, nor the most bitter, kind of suffering. We will leave aside for the moment spiritual suffering. We would just draw attention here to those painful experiences that come to us by the unfaithfulness or coldness of those we love, by the loss of friends, by all those slights and hurts we are bound to receive from time to time and which often penetrate into the very depths of our hearts.

Why is it that sometimes just those friends for whom we have done the most, to whom we have given innumerable marks of affection, requite us with coldness and seem to have forgotten all we have done for them? Why is it that, just at the moment when we are in a bad state and look desperately for an understanding soul, we find none? At such times, it is difficult, indeed, not to become bitter. Yet this is precisely what we must avoid at all costs. And the easiest way to do it is to turn again to our Lord. Where was there a man for whom He had done more than for Peter? Yet even Peter failed to understand what Jesus had so patiently tried to teach him for three years, and in the end, just at the moment when, humanly speaking, the Master needed him most, Peter even denied having known Him.

And what shall we say of the ten lepers who were healed and did not even say thank you — all except one, and he a Samaritan?[34] What shall we say of the rich young man whom He had singled out with a special affection, but who turned his back on Him because he preferred material things to Divine Love?[35]

[34] Luke 17:11-19.
[35] Matt. 19:16-22.

Learn to benefit from your sufferings

If we desire to lead the Christ life, we must also accept its sufferings and accept them, as far as in us lies, in the Christlike spirit.

But there is another side to this suffering from human coldness and ingratitude. Our Lord's sufferings were perfectly pure; He, the utterly unselfish Giver of all good things, was refused and He suffered because men whom He longed to save would not let Him do so. But with us it is different. Our human affections are mingled with so much selfishness, with so much desire for our own satisfaction, that they need to be purified. Moreover, these affections often prevent us from going straight to God.

We read in the lives of the saints how they were opposed by those whom they had considered their warmest supporters, or how their trusted directors were suddenly removed, so that they were left alone with all their difficulties in order to lean on God alone. These periods of utter loneliness and lack of human response are really our great opportunities. For when we are empty of human affections, left alone in the void, so to speak, and accept this void without bitterness and with humble resignation, God can come and work in us as He wills. This divine work will produce great purity in our affections; we shall emerge from the periods of loneliness, of misunderstandings and hostility far less selfish, far more ready to accept friendship in the right way; that is to say, as a gift from God that we value, but to which we do not cling, and which we shall use not so much to our own advantage as for the good of those whom we love. It is the wrong way of clinging to a human being, of expecting from him what only God can give, that makes a thorough purification of our human relationships imperative, and this purification is brought about most effectively by just these sufferings from coldness and misunderstandings.

Let us, then, instead of being harassed and perturbed by suffering, receive it lovingly as the Cross that Christ Himself has bidden us to take up. It is the sign of our Faith; and it is not cold and hard and dismal. For it is the Tree of Life; and, if we will accept it, it will blossom forth into the glories of Christian joy, of a joy which, as our Lord Himself has promised, no man will be able to take from us.[36]

[36] John 16:22.

Chapter Six

☙

Be joyful

"These things I have spoken to you, that my joy may be in you, and your joy may be filled."[37] "And your joy no man shall take from you."[38] "Ask and you shall receive, that your joy may be full."[39]

In the last discourse our Blessed Lord addressed to His disciples immediately before His Passion, He promised joy to them. He promised it not once, but many times; and He promised not a passing, ephemeral joy, but a joy that no man would take away — no man, not even those who would kill Him the very next day or those who would lead them to martyrdom in the years to come. That the promise was fulfilled we know; for we read in Acts that "they indeed went from the presence of the council, rejoicing that they were accounted worthy to suffer reproach for the name of Jesus."[40] And from the days of St.

---

[37] John 15:11.
[38] John 16:22.
[39] John 16:24.
[40] Acts 5:41.

Stephen, who, "looking up steadfastly to Heaven, saw the glory of God and Jesus standing on the right hand of God,"[41] to our own days, when Fr. Maximilian Kolbe[42] died in a Nazi hunger bunker, after months of unspeakable tortures, his face shining and radiant with joy — joy has been the sign of the Christian saint, joy that defies all suffering, joy that not even the diabolical torturers of our own age can take away.

Nietzsche, the atheist German philosopher, once taunted Christians because, although they believed in Redemption, their faces hardly ever showed a "redeemed" expression. It was Nietzsche's tragedy that he knew Christianity only as it presented itself in certain narrowminded and bigoted cliques of Protestantism.

Yet are we ourselves quite without fault in this matter? Do we radiate joy as we should if we would be true followers of our Lord, the Giver of joy?

We sometimes enter a room or a church where there are gathered together groups of people making a special effort to lead a real Christian life; let us say Children of Mary, a young men's sodality, a chapter of tertiaries, or an assembly of retreatants. From the looks on their faces, we might gather that they were creditors attending a bankruptcy court who had just heard the news that they had lost all their investments.

---

[41] Acts 7:55.

[42] St. Maximilian Kolbe (1894-1941), Franciscan priest who was imprisoned at Auschwitz, volunteered to take the place of a married man who was chosen for execution, and, after being starved for two weeks, was executed by lethal injection.

Sometimes it requires a truly heroic effort to preserve a normal and happy expression on our face if we look down a table of ladies or gentlemen engaged in the feeding process during a retreat. Why, oh why, does no one ever smile, and, if we attempt courageously to smile at our neighbor, why do we receive only a pained and disapproving look by way of reply? In fact, a young and very devout Catholic once blamed a much older and no-less-devout friend that she entered a church as if she went "to a party," whereas the younger girl would never raise her eyes from the ground nor allow a smile to lighten her features while she was in church.

But is that really how we should behave in our Father's house? It is, of course, right and proper to be recollected in church and not to look around, wondering who is there, or to exchange the latest news with our next-door neighbor. But, surely, recollection does not imply stern rigidity, nor should it prevent us from expressing fraternal charity by a smile to a neighbor or a friend.

It is the gracious custom in certain very austere contemplative orders that, on taking one's place in choir, one bows right and left to one's neighbors. For when we come to church, we come to worship God — not just ourselves alone, but in common with our fellow Christians. "Behold how good and how pleasant it is for brethren to dwell together in unity" chants the psalmist;[43] and if it is good and pleasant to live in union with our brethren, we should express our pleasure at meeting them by a smile or even by a whispered "How are you?" if, for

[43] Ps. 132:1 (RSV = Ps. 133:1).

example, we know someone to have been ill or otherwise in trouble. For charity comes first; and true recollection is by no means incompatible with taking account of others' needs — and we all need the smile of Christian love — although it is incompatible with taking account of others' faults.

Indeed, it is the greatest compliment to be told that we come into church as to a party, for it shows that Mass and prayer are not burdensome duties to us but the joy of our life. God Himself means us to be joyous in His service. Did not Christ rise on the third day? Does not the Church chant *Alleluia* on every Sunday except in Lent? Are we not a royal race, the race of the redeemed? Is not the Bridegroom with us in our tabernacles; more, in our very souls? And should we sit frowning and gloomy when we are assembled to hear His word?

Christianity is not the religion of suffering; it is the religion of suffering vanquished, turned into triumphal joy. The pivot of the Church's year is not Good Friday but Easter Day; the Apostles were not so much witnesses of His death as of His Resurrection.

Perhaps it is time to stress this great and wonderful truth more emphatically in these days, when it seems that so many of our fellowmen know no longer the meaning of suffering and, as a corollary, mistake pleasure for joy. Now, the principal difference between these two is that pleasure has its seat in the senses and, hence, is easily destroyed, whereas joy resides in the soul and can endure even if the body is afflicted with pain. If, moreover, the soul is truly Christian and its joy is centered in Christ, joy will be all-powerful, overcoming even the severest sufferings both of body and mind.

Why is it that the saints are so lovable, that men almost instinctively flock to them? Surely one of the chief reasons is that they radiate joy, helping their brethren to bear the sufferings of this world more easily. We need not go back to bygone times; we need only think of the marvels accomplished by those holy priests and laymen whose presence in concentration camps was the one bright ray of light that made the horrors of such existence not only endurable, but a source of graces that may yet bring the Faith back to an apostate world.

These are the heights to which supernatural joy may rise in the saints. But we, beginners in the spiritual life, cannot hope to scale them at once; we have the humbler task of presenting a smiling face to those around us even if we do not feel in the mood for it; of taking part in the gaiety of others even if we have a headache; of returning the smile of a person whom we dislike, or, preferably, of smiling at him first. These seem easy things to do; and it is true, they are easy in themselves. Only when we begin to follow this course of action each and every day shall we soon realize that it needs constant effort and vigilance; for only by trying to practice constantly the "discipline of the smile," as we might call it (which, by the way, was one of the principal means of sanctification used by Thérèse of Lisieux), shall we realize what a very difficult achievement it is.

Of course, by this we do not mean an insipid or hypocritical smile, but a smile that is the outcome of a life striving for ever more intimate union with our Lord. For, if we are united to Him, we give Him our will and all our desires and, hence, are enabled to find peace and happiness even in adversity, knowing that this, too, is His will and meant for our sanctification. Therefore, although we may be hurt and suffer a great deal, it will not take away that supernatural happiness which is God's gift to Christians.

The saintly youth Pier Giorgio Frassati,[44] one of the most influential members of Catholic Action in Italy after the First World War, and an excellent sportsman who sought — and found — perfection in a perfectly normal life in the world, wrote these lines after giving up the girl he wanted to marry in deference to his parents, because, in his view, "to destroy one family in order to create another would be sheer folly." "You ask me," he writes to his sister, "whether I am in good spirits. How could I not be so, so long as my trust in God gives me strength to be happy? We should always be cheerful. Sadness should be banished from all Christian souls. For suffering is a far different thing from despondency, which is the worst of all diseases. It is almost always the product of unbelief. But the purpose for which we have been created shows us the path along which we should tread, strewn, maybe, with many thorns, but not a sad path. Even in the midst of intense suffering, it is one of joy."[45]

There seems to be a special need in our time to stress the note of joy in every authentic Christian life, a joy that does not exclude, but embraces suffering. For there is a tendency,

---

[44] Bl. Pier Giorgio Frassati (1901-1925), young Dominican tertiary devoted to the Eucharist and to helping the poor; known as the "Man of the Beatitudes."

[45] H. G. Hughes, *Pier Giorgio Frassati* (London, 1933), 104 ff.

even — or perhaps especially — among Catholic writers, to depict the Christian life as one of fear and restraint: the poor sinful creature struggling in vain against the evil tendencies of his nature, tormented by the fear of the consequences of his sins, yet powerless to extricate himself from the fateful net in which he finds himself enmeshed, and finally ending in despair. Now, this is precisely what the Christian life is *not*. The joy of the Christian life is that, however weak our poor human nature may be, the grace of God is strong and is always there to help us. Through the virtue of hope infused into our souls at Baptism, we are enabled to rise again after each fall, however serious. Only if we commit the ultimate sin against this virtue and despair of the goodness of God shall we be cut off irrevocably from the life of grace and thus from eternal salvation.

Whatever novelists may tell us to the contrary, a joyless life ending in despair is no Christian life at all; and grace for our conversion is normally given already in this life, not at the moment of death after a life of fully conscious sin. To depict the Christian life — as seems to be the fashion of the moment — as one lived in fear of a threatening eternity without our being able to avert the threat and to give up sin is to mistake its meaning altogether. "Fear not"[46] is one of the refrains of our Lord's teaching, for love casts out fear and gives joy. The Christian life is a life of joy precisely because it is a life of the love of God, not of the fear of Hell.

It is no mere accident that, according to statistics, the number of Catholics frequenting psychoanalysts' consulting

[46] Cf. Matt. 10:31, 17:7.

rooms should be lower than that of Jews and Protestants. God-centered Christian joy is incompatible with neurosis, whereas self-centered pleasure may easily lead to it.

Perhaps some of our readers may find all this too simple. Work and recreation, suffering and joy, love of God and love of our neighbor — we seem to refuse to take any notice of all the complications that "the modern mind" is so apt to discover in itself as well as in its relationship to its fellows and the world. And are not these complications far more interesting and far more important than those simple things we have mentioned and the simple solutions we have offered?

May we therefore be allowed to say a word in defense of simplicity?

Chapter Six

⤳

Embrace simplicity

It is true that, in our age of psychoanalysis and complicated machinery, simplicity is a quality of life and character much underrated if not actually despised. Perhaps this is the reason so many of the saints recently placed on the altars by the Church for our example are men and women of striking simplicity, and even children. St. Bernadette, the Curé d'Ars, St. Thérèse of Lisieux, St. Maria Goretti — a peasant girl, a peasant priest, a young Carmelite cultivating the childlike spirit in its integrity, and a child martyr for purity.[47] It seems as if the Holy Spirit deliberately opposed simplicity to the neurasthenic complications of the modern world.

Our age is given to despise simplicity, perhaps because it is so difficult to understand and even more difficult to attain,

---

[47] St. Bernadette (1844-1879), Sister of Notre Dame who, in 1858, received eighteen apparitions of the Blessed Virgin Mary; the Curé d'Ars (1786-1859), St. John Vianney; patron saint of parish priests; St. Maria Goretti (1890-1902), twelve-year-old girl who was killed while resisting a young man's advances.

except for those in love with it. It certainly is almost impossible to define. Simplicity is poles apart from simple-mindedness in the sense of intellectual limitations. In fact, it is quite the opposite of limitation. For the sovereignly simple Being, God, is completely above our natural understanding; and even the great simple things of our daily experience — life and death, love and beauty — cannot be perfectly understood by our reason, because they are so simple; yet we know them as soon as we meet them, for they "stare us in the face."

There is a way to simplicity: "Unless you become as little children. . . . Unless a man be born again . . ."[48] It does not mean returning into our mother's womb, as Nicodemus foolishly imagined; it does not mean becoming primitive by some artificial retrograde movement. Simplicity is not the same as primitivity and is reached only by a slow, progressive (not retrogressive) transformation under the influence of the great simplifying power that theologians call *grace* and which brings forth all the good things of the true life. For simplicity is marvelously fruitful.

Take, for example, those few simple sentences that are known as the Beatitudes. "Blessed are the poor in spirit. . . . Blessed are the meek. . . . Blessed are the pure in heart, for they shall see God. . . . "[49] The most sublime way of perfection is expressed in these few bare sentences, in which there is not one superfluous word. They have provided generation after generation of saints with food for their spiritual life, and a

[48] Matt. 18:3; John 3:3.
[49] Matt. 5:3 ff.

succession of theologians from Gregory of Nyssa[50] and St. Augustine[51] to St. Thomas Aquinas and down to modern scholars like Gardeil and Garrigou-Lagrange with an inexhaustible source for their teaching on Christian perfection.

The simpler a thing is, the more universal and the more fruitful it will be. We can meditate all our lives on the Our Father and discover ever new riches in it. Or, on a lower plane, we can probe into the clear-cut articles of the *Summa* of St. Thomas Aquinas and find fresh light in them with each reading. It is the simple things that last through the centuries, that later generations develop, reinterpret, and assimilate, as food is assimilated, absorbing what nourishes them and making it their own.

Or let us take the sublime simplicity of the divine drama of the Redemption. Because man, changeable creature that he is, had offended God by his disobedience, God, in His infinite love, became man to repair the fault by His obedience. A child can understand it; in fact, a child can understand it far more readily than a grown-up person, because the child is as yet simple enough to understand the simple truths. God became man, and for His human life He chose the simplest setting: a manger, a carpenter's family, a small town in an out-of-the-way province of the Roman Empire. Fishermen and women were His followers, and His most terrifying thunders were reserved for those who made the way to God so complicated that only they themselves pretended to be able to walk in it.

[50] St. Gregory of Nyssa (d. c. 395), bishop and writer.
[51] St. Augustine (354-430), Bishop of Hippo.

Yet the way to God is very simple. "I am the Way."[52] You know not how to be united to Him, the Way that leads to the Father? Why, nothing could be simpler. You need only love Him. See, He takes the simple things of our daily meals, bread and wine, and says these simple words: "Take and eat, this is my Body. . . . Drink, this is my Blood. . . ."[53] And so you have Him within you, so you are united to Him, far more intimately than ever a woman was to her lover. Are we to be scandalized, as were so many of His followers, and leave Him because our minds, made complicated by sin, cannot grasp the simplicity of Divine Love?

If we would bring forth fruit sixty- and a hundredfold, we must feed our souls on the simple food of the Body of our Lord and of the teaching of His Church — that food marvelously designed by the Giver of all food to be assimilated by each one of us according to his capacity. The way of assimilation is the way of prayer, because it assimilates us to God Himself. It leads with wonderful efficacy from multiplicity to unity, from complication to simplicity.

We begin with laborious meditation or spiritual reading, taking point by point, sentence by sentence, pressing out its meaning as juice is pressed out of an orange. And then, if we are faithful, there will come a day when not a drop of juice will come, however hard we may press with our understanding; and the understanding itself will refuse to go on with its labors, which have become futile. On that day, however useless all

[52] John 14:6.
[53] Cf. Matt. 26:26-28.

our efforts may seem, we should rejoice, for our feet have been set on the blessed way of simplicity. Under the increasingly powerful action of the Holy Spirit, our activities are more and more unified, and slowly our whole life becomes marvelously simple.

For it is a simple thing to say, "Thy will be done" — although it may all but break our heart. The supremely simple act of giving His human will entirely to the Father cost the Son of God the Agony of Gethsemane. The fact that an action is simple does not make it easy. More often than not, the simple way of dealing with a situation will be the more difficult and costly, while the roundabout and complicated escape will be the easy way out. It is the simplicity of martyrdom; and that simplicity, too, our world has to learn anew, as our brethren have already learned it in concentration camps and before firing squads, and as all the saints have had to learn it, whether they died in their beds or on the rack. For it is only when all the complications and neuroses produced by our pampered self-will shall have been purged away by suffering — whether it be in this world or in the next — that we shall be sufficiently conformed to the Divine Simplicity to enter into the kingdom of Heaven.

Chapter Seven

~

Beware of temptations that afflict the devout

Before considering the life of prayer in greater detail, we have to clear away some of the obstacles that are wont to hinder the full development of this life. For it must be said that there are certain dangers to which the devout are especially exposed and which must at least be faced courageously, even if they cannot be overcome all at once.

It is a well-known fact that much scandal is caused and much good prevented by the lack of even ordinary human kindness, let alone of a high degree of fraternal charity, in the case of many who spend a large part of their time in church and are even daily communicants. These people also go to weekly Confession. Yet we are sometimes inclined to think that for them our Lord's words might be slightly modified: they see the mote in their eyes, but not the beam,[54] and are surprisingly ignorant of their major faults, while being aware of minor weaknesses that are not nearly so displeasing to God as are those of which they seem to take no notice.

[54] Cf. Luke 6:41.

It is not by accident that both the Mystical Doctor of the Church and she whom Pius XI called "the greatest saint of modern times"[55] should be so pitilessly insistent on detachment as the indispensable condition of any progress in the life of the soul. For it is by undue attachment, whether to our possessions, or to persons, to opinions, to occupations, or to any other things, both material and spiritual, that we are most hindered in our progress. By these attachments we are prevented not only from giving ourselves entirely to God, but also from loving our neighbor as we ought.

Let us begin with the lowest: material possessions. It is surprising how many otherwise good, devout Catholics are in the same position as the rich young man, or, rather, worse.[56] For they are normally not asked to sell all they have, but just to give away a little: to make a small sacrifice to relieve a poor family or friend; or perhaps not even that, but just to lend a trifle to someone who is in need of, say, a bed or a table. But although they may have enough and to spare, they are afraid that just this little thing might be required by themselves, and so they refuse. "So sorry, would have loved to help, but it is so difficult to get things replaced these days, and so I'm sure you'll understand." And what can the poor man or woman do but say, "Oh, it's quite all right. I'm sure I'll be able to manage," and retire in confusion.

And how many of us are never reproached by our conscience if we make undue profit from our neighbor's necessity?

[55] St. Thérèse of Lisieux.
[56] Matt. 19:16-22.

Beware of temptations that afflict the devout

Alas, men and women looked on as very devout are condemned by rent tribunals for exorbitant charges and themselves think nothing of underpaying their staff if they can find those who work extra cheap — for example, foreigners in need.

We have purposely chosen examples where a personal relationship is involved, because in these cases, the sin against justice is made all the more poignant by the fact that the virtues of fraternal charity and mercy are also violated. Yet in most of these cases, the offender will not be conscious of doing anything wrong. The reason is not far to seek. We live in a pagan society; and although we are Catholics in church, many of us have the same standards in daily life as our pagan neighbors, or even worse ones, for *corruptio optimi pessima* — "the corruption of the best is worst." But if we realize this and make a point of examining our everyday actions in this respect, we shall soon be rid of these grosser faults.

It must be admitted that it is only too easy to fall into these faults. It is so much more natural to fallen humanity to attach itself to visible creatures than to the invisible Creator. But God has provided for our needs. He has not only given us His Word in Scripture; He has given us a special saint whom we may imitate and who will help us by her most powerful prayers to overcome such foolish weaknesses. Listen to this confession of St. Thérèse of Lisieux concerning her attachment to her prioress. "I remember," she writes, "that when I was a postulant, I had often such violent temptations to seek my own satisfaction and find some drops of joy, that I was obliged to hurry past your cell and cling tight to the banisters to keep from retracing my steps. There came into my mind any number of permissions to ask, a thousand pretexts to give way to my nature and let it have what it craved. How happy I am now that I denied myself at the very beginning of my religious life."[57] If we remember that she was a young girl of fifteen at the time, the period when foolish attachments are almost inevitable, this extraordinary mastery of self is all the more admirable. That her memory did not deceive her in this respect is borne out by a letter, written in January 1889, in which she says, "Since I can find no created thing to content me, I will give all to Jesus; I will *not* give a creature even an *atom* of my love."[58] This, of course, is not to be taken literally, for her letters are overflowing with love and affection for her family and her fellow religious. It means, however, that she will not let any too sensible affection for a creature intrude into that sanctuary of her soul that is reserved for God alone.

Now, it is not so very difficult to distinguish between these different kinds of affection. If, at the time of prayer, one person always occupies our imagination; if we are constantly wondering about him, what he is doing, why he is doing this or that; if we are mortally hurt when we are not accorded the amount of attention to which we think ourselves entitled; if we find it difficult or even impossible to think about God for no other reason save that we are too preoccupied with this particular person — then we may be quite sure that this affection is not pleasing to God. If, on the other hand, we feel that the other

---

[57] St. Thérèse of Lisieux, *The Story of a Soul*, ch. 10.
[58] Letter no. 50 in the edition of Abbé Combes.

person helps our spiritual life; if, when thinking about him, we quickly forget him because we find ourselves drawn to our Lord, then there is no danger, although even so it is good to keep a watch on ourselves. Human nature is weak. How weak is realized only after many years of spiritual effort: for God does not try us beyond our strength; if He showed us our weakness right at the beginning, we should surely give up even before making a start.

Let us, then, be valiant and, with the help of God and His saints, overcome all these weaknesses of our too-selfish nature. For although they may seem trifles to us, they are in reality very serious obstacles. The spiritual life, the converse of the soul with God, is a very delicate organism, easily upset by matter that is foreign to it. If a small piece of coal dust falls on our hand, we hardly notice it; but if it penetrates into our eye, it hurts intensely and we are unable to see clearly until it has been removed. The spiritual life is far more delicate than even the eye, and these seemingly negligible imperfections can shipwreck us altogether. If, on the other hand, they are deliberately fought and overcome, they will be transformed into the means of progressing rapidly.

For we must always remember that all these faults and imperfections are the consequences of Original Sin, that no human being except our Blessed Lady is born without them. The saints have had the same temptations as we; they, too, were inclined to undue attachments, to irritation with their neighbor, to rash judgments; but by the utmost fidelity in cooperating with the graces given them — and each one of us is given many graces every day, every hour of our lives — they conquered the evil tendencies of their nature and became models of holiness for their brethren.

Our difficulties, however, do not arise only from our relationships with our neighbors. They are sometimes also due to inordinate attachment to our own views, to one-sided ideas, to a lack of balance in our judgments. We will give a few examples of what we have in mind.

The Liturgy of the Church is a wonderful thing, and a full participation in it is the ideal of a truly Christian life. Yet even devotion to the Liturgy can lead to very curious results. Sometimes it almost seems as if the Devil takes a particular pleasure in turning the most beautiful expression of the Church's love of her Lord into a snare for her children. For devotion can, in certain souls, become almost an obsession (the encyclical *Mediator Dei*[59] has some pertinent things to say about this danger), so that they are quite incapable of appreciating, or even tolerating, any other forms of prayer and worship. These souls will sneer at devotion to the Sacred Heart; they will ridicule the Holy Hour, scorn the Rosary, and despise those unfortunate fellow Christians who neither know the structure of the Mass nor have ever recited even a part of the Divine Office.

Yet the whole purpose of the Liturgy is to bring us nearer to God and to cause us to grow in love of Him and our neighbor. If, instead of making us grow in charity and humility, our love of the Liturgy causes us to despise others, there must be something wrong — not indeed with the Liturgy, but with us.

[59] Pope Pius XII's encyclical on the Sacred Liturgy (November 20, 1947).

Beware of temptations that afflict the devout

This is even more evident in the case of those who, having to attend a church where the liturgical spirit is lacking, become disgruntled and indulge in constant criticism of their priests. Instead of being the center and supreme joy of their spiritual life, the Mass will then become for them a constant source of irritation and even anger. Instead of being drawn into the orbit of the Sacrifice of Calvary, they will let their mind dwell on such externals as the shape of the vestments or the movements of the priest, and the slightest deviation from the rubrics will set their whole being throbbing with indignation. And if they are of a violent temper, they will even go and tell Father exactly what they think of him. And then, of course, peace will have gone from their spiritual life completely.

Now, it is certainly a good thing that a priest should love the Liturgy and that he should, as far as is possible in the circumstances in which he finds himself, educate his flock to an intelligent participation in it. Nor are liturgically-minded laymen to be blamed if they try, prudently and with tact, to persuade their parish priest to do this. But if a priest rejects any such proposals, then the only way that will allow us to possess our souls in peace is to accept the refusal as a mortification sent to us from God and to refrain from all bitterness and criticism.

This is a principle that should always be followed if we find ourselves in opposition to our parish priest. There are so many occasions of conflict of opinions. Nothing is more disedifying, and at the same time more upsetting, for the spiritual life than a feud with the parish priest — that is to say, with the very man who, according to the divine dispensation, distributes the sacraments to us. If we cannot live in peace with him, then surely our spiritual life is vitiated at its source.

This, of course, does not mean that we should change our opinions or that we should think everything right that he does. It means, however, that we should abstain from judgment (so difficult for most of us, yet so vital for our peace of soul) and that we should revere in him, whatever his personal faults, the representative of Christ, the "minister of the Blood," as St. Catherine of Siena would say.

This is the goal to which our love of the Liturgy should lead us: to be so penetrated with the spirit of supernatural charity that we can live in peace with all men, always ready to abandon our own judgments and preoccupations when necessary and to accept trials and contradictions in whatever form they may come.

This is indeed the greatest difficulty of the Christian life: the opposition and misunderstanding that come to us from our fellow creatures. These can be truly met only by overcoming them through the great Christian virtues of humility, patience, meekness, and charity. And in this connection we would mention just one more "pitfall" which, it seems to us, prevents certain of our contemporaries from living a full and healthy life. We mean the attraction to what is styled "the hermit life."

There are many devout people who, confronted with our neopagan society, seek the easy way out by breaking away from it altogether. Feeling what they believe to be a compelling attraction to the solitary life, they talk and even write persistently about it, and never tire of citing the Ancren Riwle,[60] and Richard Rolle[61] and Mother Julian[62] as its outstanding examples. From time to time, they also mention the Fathers of the Desert and Charles de Foucauld,[63] although much less frequently; they obviously are aware that these latter lived their extraordinary life in a manner more admirable than imitable.

Now, Aristotle says that in order to lead the solitary life, we must be either a god or a beast; but this in no way deters our modern would-be hermits. It is surely significant that the Church, although canonizing individual hermits, has never set the seal of her approval on the life as such. She has never approved either the Ancren Riwle or any other rule for the guidance of would-be anchorites. For man is a "social animal," and only contemplatives of the highest degree could practice the second great commandment of charity toward our neighbor without having any opportunity of contact with him. The Greek Fathers themselves utter constant warnings against the dangers of the solitary life, which is the one best fitted to lead both to selfishness and to all manners of illusions.

It seems, therefore, that only an outstanding vocation warrants such a life, especially in times like our own, when the Church cannot afford that her children should lose themselves

---

[60] Thirteenth-century code of rules for the life of anchoresses, which is sometimes called "The Nuns' Rule."

[61] Richard Rolle of Hampole (c. 1300-1349), hermit and writer.

[62] Mother Julian of Norwich (1342-1416), English mystic.

[63] Charles de Foucauld (1858-1916), French soldier who became a hermit in Palestine.

in daydreams about hermits, while the world cries out for people ready to lead intense lives of prayer, here and now, in the daily round of our ordinary occupations.

We cannot repeat it too often: one of the chief dangers of the spiritual life, especially as lived in the world, is the daydream. We daydream of high degrees of prayer; we daydream of martyrdom; we daydream of hermit lives. For daydreams are pleasant and easy; they cost us nothing and, consequently, are completely worthless. The smallest and most insignificant act of charity is another stone helping to build up the edifice of our supernatural life; but a daydream is something without objective existence, a figment of our fancy preventing us from using our time for the purpose for which God means it to be used.

We must, therefore, not waste that precious time which we are called upon by St. Paul to redeem. On the contrary, we should use it as fully as is possible for us; for, our lives being as crowded and harassed as they are, we can live spiritual lives only if we learn the art of making time for God.

Chapter Nine

☙

Make time for God

"How I would like to deepen my spiritual life by more prayer and reading; but I simply haven't the time."

This complaint can often be heard from many who earnestly desire a more intimate relationship with God and feel that what prevents them from achieving it is mainly lack of that minimum of leisure which is indispensable for an intense life of prayer.

Yet, if we look at the saints, we shall discover the paradoxical phenomenon that the more they prayed, the more time they seemed to have for their apostolic work. Whether we take St. Dominic[64] or the great St. Teresa, St. Bernard or St. Catherine of Siena, we are confronted with the fact that they accomplished in a very short time tasks sufficient for several ordinarily long human lives, and in addition gave what seems to us a disproportionate amount of time to prayer. It looks, indeed, as if our Lord's promise to add all else to those who seek

---

[64] St. Dominic (c. 1170-1221), founder of the Dominican Order.

first the kingdom of God includes even time.[65] If we give time to Him, He will give it back to us with interest. This may sound somewhat mysterious, but the importance of the time factor in the spiritual life will become clearer if it is first considered from the purely natural point of view.

Although the proverb says that time is money, most people are much more careful about how they spend their money than about how they spend their time. Yet the saints regard time as a gift from God, granted them in order to work out their salvation in it. There is a poignant urgency in many of the New Testament sayings on time; for example, in those words of our Lord: "I must work the works of Him that sent me, whilst it is day: the night cometh, when no man can work";[66] and of St. Paul, "See, therefore, brethren, how you walk circumspectly . . . redeeming the time."[67]

In this matter, as in so many others, the children of the world are often wiser than the children of light.[68] What is the secret of those businessmen, writers, doctors, and politicians who seem to cram into the twenty-four hours of their day three times as much as other people without appearing unduly hurried or flustered? It is easily told, but not so easily imitated: it is simply a systematically planned day in which first things are allowed to come first, with fixed hours for everything, yet sufficient elasticity to allow for unforeseen interruptions.

[65] Cf. Matt. 6:33.
[66] John 9:4.
[67] Eph. 5:15-16.
[68] Cf. Luke 16:8.

The "rule of life" recommended by spiritual directors is nothing more than such a "planned day" with special regard to the life of the soul — which is particularly necessary, because prayer and spiritual reading are so easily crowded out by other things that seem more urgent at the moment. We argue that it will be possible to find half an hour for prayers later on, and then it is bedtime, and the half hour has never materialized.

For the period (or periods) of prayer, it is therefore important to choose a time when interruptions will be least likely. For many people, this will be the early morning, the time preferred by our Lord Himself and by many saints after Him. But if this is impossible, there is always the chance of slipping into a church for half an hour after work, or before going home for dinner, or possibly during lunch hour or before going to bed. The chief thing is to set apart at least one definite period for prayer and to keep to it regularly, unless prevented by exceptional circumstances.

In addition to these set periods of prayer, there are other possibilities of making time for God. The lives of the saints are full of examples. When St. Catherine of Siena was deliberately deprived by her parents of any time for herself, she humbly endured the trial and, while it lasted, turned the most commonplace occupations into opportunities for prayer. Modern life, too, is full of such opportunities. Fr. Lamy used to say the Rosary while walking from one place to the other, visiting his parishioners. Saying the Rosary while waiting for a bus or a train, or in a restaurant queue, or while walking to and from work, and so forth, is an excellent means of fixing our mind on God, as well as of making intercession for the men and women around us, so many of whom know not "the gift of God."[69]

It is difficult at first to realize how many opportunities there are during the day for prayer. Although often no more than a few seconds, they will suffice for a quick thought of God. And He whose delight is to be with the children of men[70] will not leave souls to struggle alone.

To "make time" deliberately and perseveringly, even in the face of great difficulties, is the work of man. But since God is never outdone in generosity, He will ordinarily reward faithfulness not only by progress in prayer, but also by opportunities for extending the time given to it. It is always best to take our Lord at His word. "Ask and it shall be given unto you."[71] So why not ask Him for time for prayer, provided, of course, that it be His will for a soul to pray more? Just as in St. Catherine's life, He broke down the resistance of her parents so that she was left free to pray, He may do the same for others, if He sees them determined to give all to Him.

But the gift must come from Him; it must not be snatched against His will. Neglecting the duties of our state for the sake of prayer would be the wrong way around, as we have seen, and would lead only to illusion. The soul may surely trust the Holy Spirit to take care of its sanctification, for, even if more time should not be given, He will find ways of uniting the soul to Himself more closely even in the turmoil of the world.

[69] Cf. John 4:10.
[70] Cf. Prov. 8:31.
[71] Matt. 7:7.

Generally, however, the soul will find that more time is granted, whether by a change of occupation or by a decrease of the demands of family and social life, or through similar factors.

There is also another way, although it needs prudence and the guidance of a spiritual director. It is a striking phenomenon in the lives of most mystics that they needed extraordinarily little sleep, so that, although their days may have been filled with activities, their nights were for the greater part given over to prayer.

Ordinary men and women cannot imitate them in this. But it is remarkable that even in the lower stages of contemplative prayer, once it becomes "passive," less sleep is in fact needed; and the opinion has been advanced by spiritual writers that prayer, in such cases, takes, as it were, the place of sleep. As it is "passive," reason and imagination as well as the body are at rest, and so the whole human being is refreshed, the more so as the soul during the time of prayer is close to the Source of all life and refreshment.

Here we touch on the most mysterious aspect of the time factor in the spiritual life: its relation with eternity. For the praying soul is in immediate contact with the Eternal; and the closer the union, the stronger the impact of eternity on the human being. It is due to this impact that the soul in the higher states of the life of prayer (in full union and ecstasy, to use the established Teresian terms), loses all consciousness of time, not as one absorbed in interesting work or reading — for there the loss is due to the effort of concentration, and despite it, the person is always conscious of existing in time — but because it is invaded by another mode of being, by the time-less, by eternity.

This invasion of the human soul by eternity may perhaps offer an explanation of the extraordinary activities of some of the saints mentioned in the beginning of this chapter. When they first set out on their life of prayer, they make time for God, but later God makes time for them. That does not mean that He adds more hours of sixty minutes each to their twenty-four-hour day.

Time is a very mysterious thing; sometimes it seems to stretch, at other times to contract. The same hour of sixty minutes that seems incredibly short to the happy lover drags on interminably for the condemned criminal in his cell. And so — but this is put forward very tentatively and diffidently — God may in some mysterious way lengthen time for His servants, whose life is permeated by eternity, so that, filled with its power, they are able to accomplish in an hour several times the amount of work that can normally be put into it by other persons. The more contemplative prayer becomes, the more the temporal life of the human being is invaded by eternity, and, by a mysterious interplay, the time it has at its disposal is invested with something of the eternal quality of the divine.

This, at any rate, was the experience of the great bishop St. Vincent Strambi,[72] of whom Maria Winowska writes, "Prayer was his spiritual recharging (*ravitaillement*), and the time which remained to him seemed to increase tenfold. Each saint's life is

---

[72] St. Vincent Strambi (1745-1824), Passionist Bishop, missionary, and preacher.

another example for us of these 'extension hours' (*heures à rallonge*) which gain in depth and even in length in exact proportion to all that has been given as just tribute to God."[73]

If man makes time for God, God will make time for man: "Ask and you shall receive." Except for rare cases, progress in the spiritual life depends on a generous allowance of time set apart for God. As in human love, the lover expects the beloved to give him as much time for being together as is compatible with her other duties, so God expects the loving soul to be together with Him in prayer as much as its circumstances allow. And, indeed, how can it desire to be together with Him in eternity, if it has not already desired to be together with Him in time? Therefore, Holy Scripture commands us to pray always,[74] so that our souls may be so attuned to Him in time that they will need no more preparation to be united to Him forever in the eternal now of the Beatific Vision.

[73] "Saint Vincent-Marie Strambi," *Vie Spirituelle* (June 1950): 633.
[74] Cf. Luke 18:1; 1 Thess. 5:17.

Chapter Ten

Found your spiritual life on the virtues

We have discussed in the beginning the basic need of our every-day life, which is common sense. This common sense, how-ever, has to be sanctified and is, let us hope, sanctified in every baptized Christian by the theological virtues and the gifts of the Holy Spirit.[75] For on these our whole spiritual life is built, especially in the narrower sense of the life of prayer.

When we speak of that life of prayer, some of us are some-times inclined to think of it as a very special thing, all bound up with wonderful experiences, visions, and ecstasies; some-thing even that might make us unfit for "normal" life; some-thing that is all right for monks and nuns who have "nothing else to do," but not for us ordinary men and women who have to struggle on in the world, earning our living and looking af-ter our families. This view is fairly widespread. And it is en-tirely wrong.

---

[75] The theological virtues are faith, hope, and love. The gifts of the Holy Spirit are wisdom, understanding, counsel, fortitude, knowledge, godliness, and fear of the Lord.

Prayer is not something added to our ordinary Christian existence; it is its very lifeblood. Nor is it a special talent that some people possess and others not, as, say, an ear for music or some technical ability. If this were so, our Lord would not have told us "that we ought always to pray and not to faint,"[76] nor could St. Paul have written to his converts, "Pray without ceasing."[77] In fact, throughout the Scriptures, both of the Old and the New Testaments, prayer is regarded as a normal human activity, as it is in most religions and has been so regarded in most times.

It is one of the abnormalities of the modern West that, even among many Christians, prayer should be considered a specialized function of religious, whereas we ordinary citizens of the kingdom cannot be expected — nor expect ourselves — to do more than say hurriedly a few morning and night prayers and occasionally the Rosary.

Now, prayer is not a specialized activity, nor does it demand any special talent, or else our Lord and St. Paul would not have told us to pray always. God has, in fact, given us all the spiritual equipment needed for Christian prayer; all we have to do is to make use of it and thereby to develop it. This equipment is nothing else but the three theological virtues and the gifts of the Holy Spirit, which all baptized Christians in the state of grace possess. They are the foundation of our whole spiritual life; they are there to be used. The more we use them, the better shall we be able to pray. And the more we

[76] Luke 18:1.
[77] 1 Thess. 5:17.

pray, the more perfectly shall we possess them. There is a wonderful interaction between them and our prayer, each helping the other to build up a sane spiritual life.

Now, the basic virtue, without which no one can be a Christian at all, is faith. "Faith," we are told in the letter to the Hebrews, "is the substance of things to be hoped for, the evidence of things that appear not."[78] Does it not almost sound like a deliberate challenge to our "scientific" age? Things that are seen and heard, things that can be investigated with precision instruments, that can be demonstrated by experiment — things, in short, toward which our senses can be turned in one way or another — these are not the object of this fundamental virtue, but things that are "only" hoped for, that do not appear; in other words, things that are completely removed from the senses and, hence, from all scientific investigation.

And with this, faith is withdrawn entirely from the competence of science because faith touches the cause of all things, God Himself, who is an object of faith precisely because He cannot be reached by the senses. It is true, He can be attained to by reason; for we can prove His existence and certain of His attributes, such as omnipotence and omniscience. But the senses cannot even go thus far; and reason itself is brought to a standstill once these basic facts have been proven. We can admire this First Cause and Mover of the Universe from afar, but neither our senses nor our reason can put us in touch with Him. For this we need faith, "the substance of things to be hoped for, the evidence of things that appear not."

[78] Heb. 11:1.

If the sacred author calls faith the "substance," he means, as St. Thomas Aquinas tells us, that by the assent of faith, we already have a first beginning of these things within us. And thus it is through faith, as St. John of the Cross repeats again and again, that we are in contact with God, with the Blessed Trinity, with our Lord, the God-Man, with our Lady, and with the whole court of Heaven. We touch all these mysteries by faith, as we shall hereafter attain to them by vision. Therefore, faith is the foundation of our whole life of prayer.

Now, if we accept this, as we are bound to do, certain practical consequences follow. The first is that we shall not be able to complain that we have no "gift" for the spiritual life. For the gift of faith is *the* one indispensable condition for a sound life of prayer. Any natural gifts, such as imagination, power of concentration, and quick intelligence, are purely secondary; they may help, but they are not necessary for the life of prayer. In fact, a too-active imagination or a too-subtle intelligence may sometimes even become a hindrance and have to be purified by the direct action of God. But of faith we can never have enough; the deeper our faith, the deeper will be our prayer.

If we realize fully what faith is, that it is dark, and that its object is the truths of our religion which are above, although not against, our understanding, we shall avoid a danger not quite infrequent in the lives of many of the devout. For faith is the foundation on which our spiritual life must be built — but credulity is not.

By *credulity* we mean the ready acceptance we give, and the inordinate importance we attach, to all manner of extraordinary happenings and alleged miracles, apparitions, and the like. Miracles indeed will always happen in the Church, and it is right and proper that we should admire them. But, more often than not, it is not the miracles approved by the Church that attract us, but unsubstantiated tales of abnormal occurrences and visions, which we accept and recount readily, and which play a much larger part in our imagination than is good for the balance of our spiritual life. All these things are, at best, embroideries, so to speak; they are not of the substance of our belief. If we rely on them too much, if we use them to reassure us that what we believe is true, instead of adhering in the darkness of faith to the truths of Divine Revelation, our whole prayer life will become lopsided; and in the time of temptation, belief in such pious stories will prove no bulwark against the wiles of the Devil. In fact, they may well become snares enticing us away from God, from the things unseen, to the visible and sensible, and so will damage our faith rather than strengthen it.

For although faith is a gift from God, it is liable to decrease as well as to increase. And if preoccupation with strange happenings may well be a danger to it, the opposite effect will be produced by applying our minds to the doctrines of the Church. It is false humility for us to say, "I am not clever enough to understand theology. I leave that to the priests." More often than not, this is only mental laziness and lack of interest. If we really love our Lord, we shall surely want to know more about Him; we shall try, as far as we are able, to penetrate into that tremendous mystery of the two natures in the one Person. Not that we can ever understand it (as little as even the greatest theologian), but if we have faith, we shall want to approach it as nearly as in us lies, for faith seeks understanding. Theology is not the prerogative of priests, although it is essential to their office that they should know theology; it is necessary for any layman desiring to lead a spiritual life. Does not the Church teach even small children theology? What else is the catechism? There we learn already that Jesus Christ is one divine Person in two natures, that the Holy Eucharist is both sacrament and sacrifice, that the likeness to the Blessed Trinity in the human soul consists in the soul's three powers of memory, understanding, and will, and many other theological truths. Surely the Church teaches us these, not to learn and accept them and then to forget all about them, but to make them truly our own by meditation and reading, so that our understanding of them will grow continually.

We so often meet Catholics who, although grown-up in everything else, have never grown up in the Faith, because they have given it no opportunity, so to speak, to grow with them. It is as if a child had learned the ABCs and read his primer, and after that never read another book. By the time he had grown up, he would have all but forgotten his letters and be practically illiterate. How many of us are thus illiterate in the Faith, knowing still the main doctrines, but without a true understanding!

Our spiritual life will be transformed, will bear unhoped-for fruit, if we only will take the trouble to nourish our faith by a more intense occupation with Christian doctrine. Compared with the majestic truths unfolding before the eyes of our mind, enlightened by the pupil of holy Faith, as St. Catherine of Siena would say, the pious tales of signs and wonders to which we were formerly attached will soon seem insipid to us, and we shall steadily grow in the virtue that is "the substance of things to be hoped for, the evidence of things that appear not."

In this definition there is already mentioned the second of the theological virtues: hope. It seems that this virtue is sometimes very much misunderstood and little practiced — not consciously anyway. It has even appeared to people — especially to those outside the Church, but also to certain oversubtle minds within — as if it were no virtue at all but, rather, selfishness, detracting from the "pure love" of God that looks for no reward, not even for the eternal possession of the Beloved. But in the New Testament, we find no trace of such a doctrine. Every single one of the Beatitudes contains the promise of a most wonderful reward: "Blessed are the poor in spirit: for theirs is the kingdom of Heaven. . . . Blessed are the clean of heart: for they shall see God. . . . Blessed are you when they shall revile you and persecute you . . . for your reward is very great in Heaven."[79]

Our Lord never asks virtue from us without promising a supernatural recompense. This, surely, cannot be just a sop to our natural selfishness! Our Lord came to cast out selfishness. If He promises us the eternal possession of God, it is because this is the exact opposite of selfishness, the perfect self-giving to the Divine Being, which, it is true, constitutes our beatitude. But this beatitude is not self-chosen; it is the will of God in our regard; it is the selfless bliss of the rational creature that has attained to the very goal for which it was created.

[79] Matt. 5:3 ff.

If we were to pretend that it is more perfect not to hope for this reward, we would actually be resisting the will of God, which is that we should hope for it; we would presume to be more selfless than St. Paul, who wrote, "If in this life only we have hope in Christ, we are of all men most miserable. If (according to man) I fought with beasts at Ephesus, what doth it profit me, if the dead rise not again? Let us eat and drink, for tomorrow we shall die."[80]

It is true, some saints have occasionally protested that they were ready even to go to Hell, if such were the will of God, in order that there might be at least one soul in Hell who would love Him. But these are no more than exaggerated protestations of love that cannot be taken literally; for the saints who made them knew very well that Hell means by definition the complete absence of the love of God, and hence cannot be desired by anyone who loves Him.

We are, then, bound to hope for the possession of God; for, as St. Thomas tells us, "The good for which we must hope properly and principally from God is the infinite good . . . but this good is eternal life, which consists in the enjoyment of God Himself."[81]

For this good we must hope throughout our life. Even if we have lost it because we have fallen into mortal sin, we know that God desires nothing more than to restore it and that we can obtain His forgiveness at any moment if we are truly sorry and confess. And even if there should be no opportunity for

---

[80] 1 Cor. 15:19, 32.
[81] *Summa Theologica*, II-II, Q. 17, art. 2.

confession at all, He will be content with an act of perfect contrition.

The one most terrible sin is the sin of despair: despair of the Lord's mercy, of His desire to forgive sin and His power to grant us grace to avoid sin — that despair of which St. Thomas says that it is in a sense even more dangerous than infidelity and the hatred of God, because, if hope be taken away, we are without resistance delivered over to all evil.[82]

As we have already had occasion to observe in our chapter on joy, it is one of the most disturbing signs of our time that there should be Catholic writers who owe their popularity among Catholics as well as among non-Catholics to novels whose main theme is their heroes' loss of faith and eventual suicide. They do not admit, however, that this supreme sin must necessarily cut off a soul from the mercy of God. It is true, our feeble human mind can never form an adequate conception of the mercy of God. Yet we sometimes wish that these authors would also show that His mercy is capable of operating effectively on sinners not only in the split second before suicide, but during life, giving a man grace to repent and live henceforth "in newness of life."[83] This is the message of the gospel; this is the foundation of our hope — and not that we are defenselessly delivered over to our instincts until we poison or shoot ourselves.

Hope, however, is not an "easy" virtue, and this is why the scholastic theologians, under whose dry precision is hidden so

---

[82] *Summa Theologica*, II-II, Q. 20, art. 3.

[83] Rom. 6:4.

much fruitful wisdom, defined its object as the *bonum arduum*, the good that is difficult to attain.[84] In current language, *hope* really means not much more than expectation. We hope that a friend will come to see us, or that a customer will send us a check, or that there will be fine weather tomorrow.

But this is not hope in the theological sense. Hope is at once more difficult and more certain. It is difficult, because its object, the eternal beatitude of the possession of God, is beyond the grasp of our senses, our reason, and our imagination and can be grasped only by hope. And it is certain, because it is guaranteed by God Himself. He Himself has revealed that He will give Himself to us as our reward. Therefore, we can be absolutely certain that He will do so. The only uncertainty that comes in is due to our own sinful nature, which may prevent us from achieving the hoped-for end by making us unworthy of it.

And this uncertainty is the wholesome antidote which prevents hope from degenerating into presumption.

Our time needs hope as much as it needs peace. It may be fruitful to consider for a moment how closely these two seem to have been connected in the mind of St. Paul. He reminds his Ephesian converts that they "were at that time without Christ, being aliens from the conversation of Israel and strangers to the testament, having no hope of the promise and without God in this world. But now in Christ Jesus, you, who some time were afar off, are made nigh by the blood of Christ. For He is our peace, who hath made both one."[85] Having no hope,

---

[84] *Summa Theologica*, II-II, Q. 40, art. 1.
[85] Eph. 2:12-14.

being without God; being in Christ Jesus and having peace: these two pairs are contrasted. For we have peace because we have hope; hope not in some spurious world peace, but in the One who loved to greet His disciples with those blissful words: "Peace be with you. . . . Fear not." For the peace He gives is founded on that theological virtue of hope, which is quite independent of human disappointments and which, in fact, flourishes in adversity.

If the misery of the world around us threatens to put fear into our feeble hearts, there is no better tonic than those glorious words of the much-tried apostle: "Being justified, therefore, by faith, let us have peace with God, through our Lord Jesus Christ, by whom also we have access through faith into this grace wherein we stand, and glory in the hope of the glory of the sons of God. And not only so, but we glory also in tribulations, knowing that tribulation worketh patience; and patience trial; and trial hope; and hope confoundeth not: because the charity of God is poured forth in our hearts, by the Holy Spirit, who is given to us."[86]

"We glory also in tribulations." It seems impossible to human nature to do so. Still, there is not only the assertion of St. Paul to convince us, but the whole history of the martyrs and the other saints of the Church to prove the truth of his words. He himself tells us the origin of this strange phenomenon of Christians actually glorying in what causes other men dejection: its root is the divine grace that is in our souls through faith. If we have the firm hope that after the trials of this life,

[86] Cf. Rom. 5:1-5.

we shall be received into the everlasting dwellings, how can we give way to downheartedness?

It is true, our sensibility is easily affected; it is almost inevitable that we should from time to time be assailed by fears — did not our Lord show Himself to us in His agony, His soul sorrowful even unto death? — but what are merely human emotions in the presence of the theological virtues? We have the most effective weapon to conquer our fears: we have hope, hope "which confoundeth not; because the charity of God is poured forth in our hearts."

For hope can be truly effective only when it is animated by charity — charity, the queen of the virtues, which is greater even than faith and hope, and whose presence in the soul is never without the other two. We all know the thirteenth chapter of the first letter to the Corinthians almost by heart; in fact, we know it so well that we hardly know it at all. For if we knew it with true comprehension, would not our lives be different from what they are? Would not our standards, our judgments, and our relationships with other people be far otherwise?

First, St. Paul makes a clean sweep of all those things which the Corinthians — and, alas, most of us — hold in such high esteem. Eloquence, prophecies, and the knowledge of mysteries — all that goes for nothing. Gifted preachers or nuns who think they have received private revelations do not seem admirable in themselves to the Apostle of the Gentiles. But he is only just beginning. Am I even a worker of stupendous miracles? That doesn't mean anything. But surely if I give all my goods to the poor? Worth nothing, says St. Paul, unless I have charity. A last bid: martyrdom, delivering my body to be burned. No. Not even that. One thing, and one thing only: charity.

The works of charity must surely be tremendous, then, if they cannot be outweighed even by martyrdom. And now we come to this amazing enumeration of quite small, insignificant things: "Charity is patient, is kind; charity envieth not, dealeth not perversely, is not puffed up; is not ambitious, seeketh not her own, is not provoked to anger, thinketh no evil; rejoiceth not in iniquity, but rejoiceth with the truth; beareth all things, believeth all things, hopeth all things, endureth all things."[87] Nothing more? Just these inconspicuous little actions and dispositions? Yes, precisely these. In these the whole Christian life consists; it is by these that we shall be judged. "At eventide they will examine you on love," wrote St. John of the Cross. And the whole life of her whom Pius XI called "the greatest saint of modern times" consisted of nothing but these small acts of charity. To do them, we need have neither great intellectual gifts nor favorable surroundings, neither riches nor social position, neither health nor beauty, no particular profession or race or temperament. Whoever we may be and wherever we may be, we can always and everywhere practice charity. For the commandment of charity is universal; and the Lord would not give a universal command unless it could be universally carried out.

But that it can be carried out by everyone does not mean that it is easy. St. Paul's extreme simplicity and homeliness in

[87] 1 Cor. 13:4-7.

this chapter are deceptive. The very first clause is enough to convince us of that: "Charity is patient." How many times every day are we tempted to be impatient — from taking our place in a line, or having to deal with a somewhat dense person, to bearing a long-drawn-out illness ourselves or nursing someone else through it?

"Charity is kind." Oh yes, it is not too hard to be kind to our friends, but to be kind to everyone, kind always, however overworked or tired we may be?

"Charity envieth not." Even if others have a comfortable home and we are without one; even if others have a well-paid job and we find ourselves out of work.

"Charity dealeth not perversely, is not puffed up." Yet how often are we tempted to give ourselves airs the moment we think we have a little authority? There we are, trying our best to lord it over others, to interfere; sometimes in the very name of charity, making our help dependent on their acceptance of our advice. But this is not true charity, which "is not ambitious, seeketh not her own."

It is so natural to fallen human nature to be ambitious, to want things — whether riches or power, whether honor or influence; and not only these worldly ambitions, but the far more dangerous spiritual ones, just those things which St. Paul rejected a moment ago unless they are accompanied by charity. "Charity seeketh not her own." Charity seeks the honor of God and the good of our neighbor.

Nor is it provoked to anger; neither does it think evil. It is difficult enough not to speak evil — but not even to think it! To check ourselves immediately if we are inclined to put an adverse interpretation on people's doings; not to give way to anger even if we are provoked by others, or, more difficult still, by our own violent temperament. We must remember that the man who wrote this was himself anything but phlegmatic; and that this whole wonderful description is the picture of the full flowering of a supernatural virtue, achieved by grace aiding constant human effort — not the picture of a somewhat weak and sleepy character which, if regarded quite superficially, some of the expressions the apostle uses might fit as well.

But the next sentence removes any such misconception. "Rejoiceth not in iniquity, but rejoiceth in the truth." Here it is that charity parts company with qualities that, especially in our days, are often mistaken for charity — namely, with the wrong sort of tolerance, whether of sin or of error; with skepticism, for which there is either no truth at all or a truth that, although it exists, cannot be found and hence cannot be rejoiced in; with weakness that is ready to sacrifice whatever convictions it may have for the sake of a false "peace and concord." And therefore, if St. Paul goes on to say that charity "beareth all things, believeth all things, endureth all things," these "all things" have to be qualified by truth. For charity will never believe what is false, but only what is in accordance with truth. And, again, it will not hope for any daydreams to come true, but only for the promises made by Truth. And so it rejoins faith and hope, without which charity cannot be in man as long as he lives on this earth.

These three theological virtues — theological, because they direct and join us to God immediately — are infused into each one of us at Baptism, and the spiritual life consists in the growth of these virtues. It can never be sufficiently stressed that it is they that make up the spiritual life — not what are commonly called "mystical phenomena," ecstasies, visions, and the like, which the Corinthians esteemed so highly that the apostle felt obliged to set forth charity as the one great object toward which all our efforts and desires should be directed. Phenomena are sometimes due to grace, but at other times, they may be caused by an abnormal psychological constitution. In each case, they have to be tested by virtue, not virtue by them. Therefore, St. Paul tells us to be "zealous for the better gifts,"[88] those which neither the Devil nor a neurotic temperament can counterfeit — that is to say, for the theological virtues and the gifts of the Holy Spirit.

These latter, which are infused into the soul at Baptism together with the theological virtues, are enumerated by Isaiah. They are "the spirit of wisdom and of understanding, the spirit of counsel and of fortitude, the spirit of knowledge and of godliness . . . the spirit of the fear of the Lord."[89] This sevenfold gift, as the hymn *Veni Sancte Spiritus* ("Come, Holy Spirit") calls it, has been commented by the greatest theologians from St. Augustine to St. Thomas and from St. Thomas to his modern interpreters, like Garrigou-Lagrange.

In fact, these gifts, which are designed to enable us to react more promptly to all the inspirations of the Holy Spirit, reach their full development only in the "passive," the properly contemplative, stage of the spiritual life, with which we are not

[88] 1 Cor. 12:31.
[89] Isa. 11:2-3.

dealing in this book. But we would emphasize that these, too, have nothing to do with extraordinary phenomena. Their principal object is to lead us to a closer relationship with God by making virtuous acts easier (as, for example, by the gift of fortitude), by enlightening our intelligence (by wisdom and understanding), and by aiding us to assist our neighbor (by the gift of counsel).

But although these gifts, as we have said, will become fully active only in the later stages of the spiritual life, they are present in our souls all the time and will make themselves felt when they are especially needed. Thus, the young neophyte who is only beginning his Christian life may yet count on the gift of fortitude if God calls him to martyrdom; and the "average" Christian to whom a friend turns in urgent need of help may sometimes be favored with an exercise of the gift of counsel far beyond his ordinary spiritual capacities.

These gifts, present at first only in germ, will develop with the growth of our prayer and will, in their turn, deepen our prayer. For in the spiritual organism, as in the physical one, there reigns the law of reciprocity. As the growing body wants to use the strength it has in exercise and, through exercising it, increases it, so the Christian soul desires to use the virtues and the gifts and, by using them, will cause them to grow in depth and vigor. Therefore, as we said in the beginning of this chapter, the more we grow in prayer, the more we shall grow in the virtues and the gifts; for prayer is the lifeblood of the spiritual organism.

⌒

Chapter Eleven

Seek a wise spiritual director

All spiritual writers agree that the person who wants to lead an interior life should have a director. Perhaps it might be asked why this should be necessary. After all, the spiritual life, or the life of prayer, is a matter entirely between God and the soul. In contrast to the sacramental life of the Church, which is mediated by the priesthood, no intermediary is required where "the lifting up of the heart and mind to God" is concerned.

Now, the spiritual director is certainly not an intermediary, but, as his name says, he is a guide. The very metaphors we often use for the spiritual life imply the necessity of a guide. For whether we think of it as a mount to be ascended, as did St. John of the Cross, or as a sea on which we launch out, as did St. Catherine of Siena, we are at once reminded that mountaineers have to take guides if they want to climb a particularly difficult peak and that ships require a pilot to bring them safely into port. So also the spiritual life, supremely important and infinitely more different from our ordinary material life than either mountains or sea, needs an experienced guide to prevent the soul from falling into many dangers.

But, it may be argued, the spiritual life, precisely because it is spiritual, needs the Holy Spirit Himself, and no one else, for a guide. How can a mere fallible human being be entrusted with such a delicate task? Now, it is perfectly true that the Holy Spirit is the one supreme guide of the spiritual life; for it is He who moves the soul, who gives it inspirations. Before every great decision the rulers of the Church have to make, they invoke the Holy Spirit.

Now, the Holy Spirit often visits the minds of the faithful; but the faithful, being immersed in the things of this world, cannot always — in fact, can only comparatively rarely — recognize His voice. For in our unregenerate consciousness, there are very many voices whispering, trying to lead us hither and thither; and it is very difficult indeed to distinguish what are but our own desires or fears, our own sudden preoccupations and moods, from what is the voice of the Spirit.

This is where the spiritual director comes in. Even in the ordinary life, a third person can often give good advice and clarify an apparently entangled situation in which we could see only difficulties and blind alleys. How much more will this hold good for the spiritual life, where a clear appreciation of the facts is so frequently hindered, not only by the natural limitations of the individual mind, but also by the effects of sin, which obscures the soul's vision in spiritual matters. Hence, we need a human guide to help us to disentangle the thicket of voices and impressions, ideas and apprehensions, and to find in it the one that is the voice of the Spirit, the will of God.

For this task, it is, of course, necessary to find the right person. If we live in a city, this is comparatively easy; among the many priests of parish churches and religious houses, there will very probably be one to meet our needs. In general, it will be necessary only to listen to the sermons of several priests and to go to Confession to them two or three times to find someone suitable. In the country, on the other hand, things will be more difficult. Perhaps the best way will be to attend retreats and days of recollection from time to time with a view to selecting a priest for our direction. If to these natural means we add the supernatural one of persistent prayer, the right guide will surely be given.

A more difficult question is what qualities to look for in a director. The needs of individual souls are different. But it is precisely a sign of the good director that he is capable of adapting himself to the requirements of very different souls: that he knows how to be gentle with the weak and timid, and firm with those needing a strong hand. He must, above all, be well versed in the ways of the spiritual life and not be addicted to his own preconceived ideas; else he will be unable to distinguish the promptings of the Holy Spirit and will substitute his personal views for them. Therefore, he must be a man of prayer and good sense and, if possible, of learning. In fact, the latter may sometimes be even more necessary than the former. This is what St. Teresa, who had the most experience in this matter, writes on the subject: "It is of great importance, then," she says, "that the director should be a prudent man — of sound understanding, I mean — and also an experienced one; if he is a learned man as well, that is a very great advantage. But if all these three qualities cannot be found in the same man, the first two are the more important, for it is always possible to find learned men to consult when necessary. I mean that learning is of little benefit to beginners, except in men of prayer."[90]

But a little later on, she modifies this statement somewhat and writes, "My opinion has always been, and always will be, that every Christian should try to consult some learned person, if he can, and the more learned this person, the better. Those who walk in the way of prayer have the greater need of learning; and the more spiritual they are, the greater is their need."[91]

By these principles, then, should the soul be guided in the quest for a director.

The story, however, does not end here. For, once a person has chosen a director, new questions will probably arise. There is first the question of obedience. We leave out of account here the "vow of obedience" to our director, for which the Church does not legislate, and which many experienced priests refuse to accept, because there is no proper authority for it and because, moreover, it will often lead souls into all manner of doubts and scruples. The case of St. Jane Frances de Chantal[92] is a classic example. An imprudent director had exacted from her a vow of obedience, and, when, after meeting St. Francis de Sales,[93] she felt attracted to him, her former director objected to the change and adduced her vow of obedience to

---

[90] *Complete Works*, I, 80.

[91] Ibid., 81.

[92] St. Jane Frances de Chantal (1572-1641), foundress of the Visitation Order.

[93] St. Francis de Sales (1567-1622), Bishop of Geneva.

himself. St. Francis de Sales had to bring into play all his wisdom and tact to extract her from an intolerable situation that was causing her great suffering.

But apart from the case of the vow, how far are we bound to obey our director?

The case is perhaps best elucidated by the example of doctor and patient. He would be a very foolish patient indeed, who, after choosing a doctor in whom he thinks he may have confidence, proceeded to doubt his diagnoses and prescriptions and to disobey his orders. Yet he is not bound to follow them; it is at his own risk and to his own detriment that he disregards medical advice.

It is the same with the spiritual director. Apart from the case in which the flouting of his advice would be contrary to a law, the director cannot exact obedience; he can only give advice. But direction would evidently be a farce if, after consultation, penitents would act according to their own lights. After all, the director has been chosen because the penitents believe him to understand more of spiritual matters than they do. So his advice should be obeyed, even if it is — and often just because it is — contrary to the wishes of the penitents.

To give an example: some penitents in their first newly found fervor may desire to give several hours a day to prayer and to do all sorts of penances. The director, however, knows from experience that such sudden enthusiasm, if not checked, is bound to lead only to a breakdown in health and probably to spiritual disaster, so that the last state of their soul would be worse than the first. He therefore limits prayer and penance to what seems a very unsatisfactory minimum.

Should those penitents, then, rather than obey, do more than they are told to do, or should they turn to another guide? Both courses would be very wrong.

Since they chose the director because he is wiser than they, they should trust him to know what is good for them. "Obedience is better than sacrifices," says the prophet.[94] And following the director's advice is better than indulging in sudden urges that may well be due, not to the promptings of the Holy Spirit, but to a very natural desire to excel — or, on a higher plane, to ill-advised generosity.

Penitents will show their mettle precisely in the way they react to such restraining direction. If they are truly supernatural, they will see in the director the human interpreter of the Divine Will and bow to his judgment. In so doing, they will perform an act of humility and obedience far more pleasing to our Lord than long hours of prayer and self-chosen penances. Moreover, if the director sees that his penitents are obedient and finds, after some time, that they are still attracted to more prayer and harder penances, taking advantage of occasions to mortify themselves in small ways, he will allow them to satisfy their desires increasingly; so that, in the end, they will have lost nothing, but gained much by their initial obedience.

There is, on the other hand, the case of the timid, or even lazy, souls who, although obviously attracted to the spiritual life, are afraid of what God might end by asking once they give in to the first demands of greater generosity. These souls evidently have to be spurred on; they will be told that getting up

---

[94] 1 Kings 15:22 (RSV = 1 Sam. 15:22).

sufficiently early for Mass will not impair their health; that depriving themselves of some material enjoyment or other will not make life dreary and dull; that we are all called to perfection, but that perfection is to be achieved only through the Cross. What are souls to do if their guide tells them such things, but they think they ought to refuse because, in their opinion, prudence (that is, concern for their health, their capacity for work, etc.) seems to justify a refusal?

Well, there is no director worthy of the name who would prevent souls from attending to the duties of their state by making excessive demands on them concerning prayer and penance. In such a case, it is almost always best to try for at least three or four weeks the regime he suggests. If, after honestly trying, we find that the practices suggested actually do undermine our health or capacity for work, the director himself will be the first to put a stop to them.

But more often than not, we will probably make the same discovery as St. Teresa, whose health improved after following the counsel of her director to do more penance. Perhaps we, too, may find that we do not feel faint during early Mass, once we have gotten used to getting up early every day; but that, on the contrary, we feel much fresher and ready to work more briskly. We may realize that a quarter hour's prayer every day, or however much it may be, does not, in fact, interfere in the least with our work or with our obligations toward our family, which, on the contrary, we shall find to improve in every way. And so, little by little, we shall allow our director to draw us out of our sloth into the life of generosity that the Holy Spirit has planned for us.

For this is the office of the director, to assist the work of the Holy Spirit in our souls. On the other hand, it is not his office to be a substitute for our own common sense, to give advice on the little details of our life that every normal person can perfectly well decide for himself, or even to help us to make up our minds on big decisions. It is of the greatest importance for a healthy spiritual development that grown-up persons should be capable of deciding such details of their life according to the rules of common sense and not to become unwholesomely dependent on their director for such things.

Nor is it within the director's province to make the great decisions of our life for us. It is very right, indeed, that, if a person has to make a far-reaching decision, he should consult his director, for most important decisions have a bearing, in one way or another, on the spiritual life. But in such a case, after weighing all the pros and cons, the director can only give his advice; he has not the power, as has a religious superior for his subjects, to make the decision himself, although it may sometimes seem to be by far the easier way out of a difficult situation to place the responsibility on the shoulders of another. But no man has the right to decide another's life unless the power is delegated to him by lawful authority, as in the case of the religious superior, or in the few exceptional cases of a particular charisma, as was given, for example, to the Curé d'Ars. In all other circumstances, the person concerned has to take the responsibility himself; no director can substitute the exercise of his free will for that person's own.

This freedom of action is involved in the very principle of spiritual direction, which would otherwise become a kind of spiritual dictation. Hence, it is preserved also when there is a question of the change of director. There are two principal reasons that justify such a change: the first is an initial mistake in our choice; the second, a spiritual development that causes us no longer to find help where we had once found it. Nevertheless, a change should never be lightly made; much thought and prayer and, if possible, the consultation of another priest should precede it. There is certainly no reason to change our director if his views sometimes differ from our own, or if he tells us things we do not like to hear. On the contrary, a change would be far more justified if a director always agreed with us and gave us the feeling of being rather wonderful people who can be fully satisfied with ourselves. On the other hand, if the director constantly, and without a really good reason, opposed our attraction to a more intense life of prayer and penance, because, as is sometimes the case, he himself was a very active person without understanding for such leanings, then, too, it would be better to make a change. But such cases will not occur very often, especially if we have been careful in our initial choice.

The second case, that of having outgrown a certain type of direction, is rather different. For just as some books on the spiritual life that had much to give us at one time may leave us cold later on, so a spiritual director who once helped us may, after some time, be no longer able to give us what we feel we need. The Church, in her wisdom, leaves her children, both religious and lay, the greatest possible freedom in the choice of their director; for, unless there is complete confidence between director and penitent, the direction would be a failure.

If, therefore, a person was honestly convinced that the priest who had helped him formerly did so no longer, he would be justified in making a change.

But here again, caution must be used. For it is quite possible for a person to imagine that he is already in the higher walks of contemplation when, in fact, he is still very much at the beginning of the way, and so his desire for a change would rest on a delusion. Again, the advice of another priest and some sound spiritual reading may settle this matter in which it is usually safer to err on the side of humility.

In fact, in most cases, a change due to the development of the soul will probably become necessary only after many years or, if a director of great wisdom and experience has been chosen, not at all. Moreover, as we advance in the spiritual life, the Holy Spirit takes charge of us more and more, as happened in the lives of so many saints whose director was removed when he was no longer needed, or another one given when the first had become insufficient.

It is not only with the saints that God deals in this way; we lesser fry, too, may confidently expect His assistance in this and other matters if we honestly try to follow His inspirations. Using, then, our own God-given common sense and following the guidance of a prudent director, we may hope one day to reach the goal that God has desired us to reach and thus to be introduced into that mansion of the Father's house that our Lord has prepared for us from all eternity.[95]

---

[95] John 14:2-3.

Chapter Twelve

☙

Take time to recollect yourself

To avoid daydreaming, the bane of the life of prayer, we need to habituate ourselves to true recollection. How is this to be achieved? Bl. Angela of Foligno[96] will tell us: "Nothing," she writes, "is really necessary for us except God. To find God means recollecting our mind in Him. And in order better to recollect one's mind, all superfluous interchange and friendship, as well as unnecessary talk, must be cut out; nor should a man desire to learn novelties; but he should rather shun all things by which the mind is distracted and begin to consider the abyss of his miseries . . . for in all the world I delight only in two things — namely, in knowing God and myself."

These words were written in the fourteenth century, when *Europe* and *Christendom* were still synonymous terms. They speak of a state of mind and soul almost unknown in our modern world, save to the few who profess to lead the contemplative life. Yet this state, which is called *recollection*, or the

---

[96] Bl. Angela of Foligno (1248-1309), Franciscan tertiary and mystic.

"gathering together" of our thoughts and desires, is perhaps more necessary now than at any other time, for it is the one means by which our age can be restored to sanity.

"Nothing is really necessary for us save God." This was at least theoretically admitted, even if not always practically acknowledged in their lives, by the men and women of Christian antiquity and the Middle Ages. Theology was then the queen of sciences. Men cared desperately for a true knowledge of God. The heated theological battles of the first centuries, the fight against Arianism,[97] Nestorianism,[98] Monophysitism,[99] as well as the medieval controversies on Platonism and Aristotelianism, nominalism, and realism — what else were they but the expression of man's profound concern with the real nature of God and of his own soul?

It is as easy as it is foolish to laugh at the fight against an *iota* carried on by St. Athanasius,[100] the heroic defender of the *homoousios*[101] against Arius; for with the absence or presence of this small letter stands or falls the divinity of our Lord and, hence, the dogma of the Trinity — that is to say, the whole Christian religion. These men, who so lived in and for

---

[97] Heresy that denied the divinity of Christ.

[98] Heresy that denied the hypostatic union — the union of the human and divine natures in the Person of Christ — and claimed that Christ was two distinct persons.

[99] Heresy that denied that Christ had two natures.

[100] St. Athanasius (c. 297-373), Bishop of Alexandria.

[101] Greek word (*homos*, "same," and *ousia*, "essence"), meaning of one essence or substance, that was used by the Council of Nicaea to express the divinity of Christ.

their Faith, knew that there is nothing really necessary for us save God.

But this truth is not even theoretically admitted by many of our contemporaries. There are quite a few things without which we profess ourselves unable to live: money or sexual love, cinema or cigarettes — all of them material. But that it should be necessary to have God seems very dubious to our pagan neighbors and is, alas, only a theoretical proposition even to many of us Catholics. We seem to have built up our lives fairly satisfactorily without Him; and even though we pay lip service to Him, we find it hard to allow Him to penetrate to the very center of our lives.

Indeed, it is not so easy to find God. For this, as Bl. Angela says, it is necessary to recollect our minds in Him. But recollection has become so difficult under modern conditions of life as to seem well-nigh impossible. There are two things essential to it: *silence* and *repose*, at least during a certain period every day. The whole technical development of the last hundred years has been increasingly detrimental to just these two: modern media, as well as all the contemporary means of travel, whether by land or by air, are sources of perpetual noise and unrest, penetrating even to the remotest corners of the earth. We are all caught up in this whirlwind, but God does not speak out of the whirlwind; His still small voice[102] cannot be heard against a background of perpetual noise and haste.

Yet these external hindrances are but the lesser enemies of recollection and can be dealt with comparatively easily when

---

[102]Cf. 3 Kings 19:11-13 (RSV = 1 Kings 19:11-13).

the bigger and more interior ones are overcome. The things that prevent it most effectively are enumerated by Bl. Angela herself: superfluous human interchange, irrelevant friendships, and unnecessary talk. They were obviously common failings in her time, as in any other, but they have increased in frightening measure in our age. The desire for constant interchange with our fellows, the living in the mass, the often almost pathological fear of being alone even if only for one evening in the week: these are symptoms that betray a complete absence of the inner life.

Technical development, again, fosters this frame of mind: if there is no human being with us, let us at least have the radio on, so that some unknown voice from the air may prevent us from entering into ourselves; or let us go to the movies and fill our minds, made for better things, with the emptiness of a foolish story of love or adventure.

Then there is the desire for knowing much, especially in the way of sensational novelties. With news broadcast throughout the day, with newspapers in the morning, at midday, and at night, we are craving information of any and every kind, however irrelevant, as long as it is news — whether it be the latest football "event," the new hairstyle of the Duchess of X, or the discovery of yet another and even more destructive instrument for killing each other. It takes a great effort to overcome this desire for knowing for the mere pleasure of "being in the know," but without quelling it, recollection is impossible. A mind perpetually hunting for ephemeral news is unable to taste the joys of resting in the Immovable and Eternal, which is God.

Take time to recollect yourself

Once a man has entered even a little way into the sphere of the Eternal — and recollection is nothing else — he will "begin to consider the abyss of his miseries." It is this that holds so many souls back from a life of recollection. We have a secret fear of the abyss that will open before us once we abandon the whirlwind and are left face-to-face with ourselves. When man, relieved for a time of all the voices shouting into his ears how wonderful he is and how great are his achievements, begins to reflect on himself, he will realize that he is not a self-contained unit, but a creature desperately dependent on innumerable other creatures, animate and inanimate, and that, in the last resort, both he and they owe their very existence to Another, a First Cause, the Source of all being. He sees himself as a creature whose life and death are under the dominion of Another, and so he begins to know not only himself but also that Other.

Then begins to dawn that light of wisdom which is the fear of the Lord. Things will gradually assume a very different aspect. For, while we realize our own weakness and dependence, we also become more and more deeply aware of the power, the wisdom, and the love of the Triune God, who desires to communicate Himself to us. With this divine power, wisdom, and love in which we begin to participate according to the measure of our creaturely love, we shall be able to make a stand against the evils threatening us. For as we enter into this divine strength that comes from recollection, we lose our fear of creatures, of events that might harm us, and at the same time that propensity to wishful thinking that is born from fear and refuses to face the facts before us. Through recollection we shall see things in their true proportion; the nightmares will vanish and also the "castles in Spain" of our daydreams. In the light of the divine reality that has entered our souls, we shall know the realities of our earthly life for what they are and, from this same light, shall receive the strength to deal with them in God's way, and not in our own, feeble, self-centered way. Then, despite the noise that is going on around us, we shall have truly found God and shall realize with an ever-deepening conviction that there is nothing that is really necessary to us save Him.

Now, this happy state of recollection is both needed for, and produced by, prayer. We need a minimum of recollection to be able to pray at all; and prayer, in its turn, will greatly contribute to a habitually recollected state of mind. It is prayer, therefore, that we have at last to approach.

Chapter Thirteen

❧

Learn to pray by praying

"Prayer," says the Greek Church Father Evagrius Ponticus[103] (in a saying repeated after him by the more famous St. John of Damascus[104]) "is the raising of the mind to God." But another definition, less well known, which was first used by Clement of Alexandria,[105] is perhaps even more satisfying. He calls prayer a conversation of the soul with God, thus bringing out more clearly the reciprocity in the act of prayer.

Now, the great question for us is how to bring about this interchange. If prayer is a conversation rather than a monologue, how are we to make contact with the partner, with God?

There are some favored souls for whom this question does not exist, because God is "there" as soon as they begin to pray. They have no more problem with talking to God than with talking to their father or brother or friend. It is not for them that this chapter is written. It would only hinder the work of

---

[103]Evagrius Ponticus (345-399), Monastic theologian.

[104]St. John of Damascus, eighth-century Church Father.

[105]St. Clement of Alexandria (c. 150-c. 215), theologian.

the Holy Spirit if they were to try any of the means suggested here for approaching God in prayer. For it is He who has approached them already without any effort on their part, and they can do no better than entrust themselves to His guidance.

There are, however, a great many souls who would like to pray, but who are at a loss as to how to set about it. The more they read about mental prayer, methods of meditation, "states," "nights," and so forth, the more confused they become. Sometimes they may even be tempted to give up before they have begun because "it is all so complicated."

The very term *mental prayer* frightens many who are under the impression that it is something very subtle and highbrow; and if they begin to hear about "composition of place" or "application of the senses," they become firmly convinced that this kind of prayer is not for them.

Now, all these high-sounding words and intricate classifications are necessary for writing books about prayer and for guiding souls in the ways of prayer. But in our approach to God, we need nothing of the kind, anymore than a child addressing his father needs a treatise on education. And perhaps one of the best "methods" — which, moreover, has the highest possible authority — when going down on our knees, is to think of God as our Father and to ask Him to make our prayer pleasing to Him.

For it is quite clear that when beginning to pray, we must think about *something*. We cannot just kneel there with our mind either a complete blank or filled with all the innumerable figments of our imagination that pass through our head all day long. We have to have some thought that will connect our mind with Him whom we are addressing, or else we are not praying, but just daydreaming — and nothing is more pernicious than that.

But this thought about God or about the things of God is nothing complicated; in fact, the simpler it is, the better it will be.

If we think of God as our Father, for example, a whole host of associations will come into our mind at once, without our having to exercise any particular cleverness or superior intelligence. *Father* — that means to most of us a being whom we trust, whom we love, who is able to protect us, who cherishes us and cares for us — and there we are in the midst of an excellent "meditation" without needing books or rules.

If such simple considerations hold our attention for the whole period of prayer, all is well; but probably this will not very often be the case. Then an excellent means of sustaining our prayer will be the old traditional method of reading some verses or chapters of the New Testament (preferably the Gospels, because they are easier to understand than the letters and bring us into more immediate contact with our Lord) or of the *Imitation of Christ*[106] or another well-tried spiritual book. In order that such reading may nourish our prayer, we must read it slowly. As soon as we have found a thought or a sentence that holds our attention and incites in us a greater love and understanding of God or of any of the mysteries of the Faith, we shall pause and let the impression sink in. If it gives us food for

[106] A spiritual classic by ascetical writer Thomas à Kempis (c. 1380-1471).

thought, we shall think about it — savor it, as it were — and not continue our reading until we feel that we need something more.

Here, too, there is nothing complicated. If we read, for example, about the multiplication of the loaves,[107] we may be drawn to admire the goodness of our Lord, who thinks even of our bodily needs. Perhaps our thoughts may stray from there to our Holy Communion that we are about to make or have already made. Quite gently, effortlessly, we shall just let our thoughts dwell on the things that attract us without doing violence to ourselves. If we cannot find anything to think about in one passage, we shall go on to another; and if the time passes without our reading having given us anything to dwell on — well, that will be God's will for us today. Perhaps tomorrow or the day after He will give us many thoughts and even feelings of love and devotion.

It is quite true that we must not attach ourselves to pleasant devotional feelings and must not seek them for their own sake. But in the beginning of the spiritual life, God will almost always give them. For we are creatures of sense, and fallen creatures at that; and as long as we are still powerfully attracted by the pleasures of sense, God in His mercy provides for us spiritual pleasures to wean us gradually from the coarser ones that we have so far indulged. Hence, we should not despise the consolations God sends us. We should gratefully accept them; but we should at the same time be very conscious that it is only because we are so weak, not because we are in

---

[107]Matt. 14:13-21.

any way advanced in the spiritual life, that God sends us these delights. As we have seen before, these feelings of love and devotion have nothing whatever to do with the high experiences the mystics describe. They have nothing to do with mystical union. They are passing attractions, "sensible consolations," as spiritual writers call them, given to us to be counterattractions to the sensuous attractions of the world.

But if we should not overestimate them, neither should we despise them. It would be a singular lack of humility if we were to reject them because we thought ourselves sufficiently advanced to be treated to the "bread of the strong." Surely God knows best what kind of spiritual diet is right for us; whatever He gives us we should accept with gratitude. For it is important that from the very outset of the life of prayer, we should be conscious that, whatever is done in prayer is the work of His grace. If we can meditate beautifully, if we are filled with happy thoughts and generous resolutions, it is not we who are responsible for these things; it is He.

And perhaps He will show His hand from time to time by allowing us to fall into some very humiliating fault in grievous contrast with all these lovely feelings that we had in prayer. When He permits this to happen, we should be deeply grateful, for it is the first step on the arduous but most salutary road to self-knowledge. On no account should we be dismayed. It would be the greatest possible mistake to say, "Well, what is the use of all this praying if I still fall into such faults as this?" The road of prayer is a long, hard, and difficult road, and generally not at all straight, but winding and roundabout. God alone knows the pace at which we are progressing. And, what is most difficult, the soul embarking on this road must not desire to know how it is advancing or at which stage of the way it has arrived. For as soon as we begin to wonder whether we are making much progress or little, whether what we are experiencing is "consolations" or "prayer of simplicity" or perhaps, rather, the "prayer of recollection" of which we have been reading in spiritual books, we have taken a wrong turn on the spiritual road.

If our mind is occupied with such considerations, if we are watching ourselves while we are praying, in order to find out exactly what we are doing, we may be quite sure that we are not praying at all, but are thinking of ourselves. This kind of introspection is the great pitfall for many who are embarking on a life of prayer, and we should strive to avoid it at all costs right from the beginning.

The most wholesome prayer is that of which we are hardly conscious. It is with spiritual health as with physical well-being: if we have a healthy body, we shall not be preoccupied with it. I never think about my nose or throat until I have a cold, or about my temperature until I have a fever. It is only the hypochondriac who will forever put the thermometer in his mouth, test his pulse, and try all variations of diet. If he reads a medical book, there is no illness that he does not imagine himself to have.

The self-conscious spiritual person is very much like the hypochondriac. He has all the "symptoms" described in spiritual books; he goes about with an invisible thermometer to take his spiritual temperature three times a day; he feels his soul's pulse assiduously; and as to trying out diets — that is to say, "methods" of spirituality — there is simply no end to his experiments.

There is, however, one important difference between the physical and the spiritual hypochondriac. His friends and family will generally laugh at the former; and that may sometimes cure him. In any case, he is not very likely to infect normal people with his strange disease. The situation is different with the spiritual hypochondriac. Very often, he will be admired for his deep spirituality, for being so well read in the mystics, so eloquent and well versed in the spiritual life — surely saintly, seeing how much time he spends in prayer! Thus, instead of realizing that all is not well with his self-centered prayer, he may easily imagine himself to be in a very advanced state and an expert on all matters of the spiritual life. Once this stage is reached, not only will a cure be very difficult, but he will also be a danger to others who come to him for advice and for discussions on the life of prayer.

The one great remedy for this is never to consider our prayer apart from ourselves and never to consider ourselves apart from God. We will make our meaning clearer. The temptation for many of us who give ourselves to prayer is to consider our spiritual life in some way objectively.

"My Spiritual Life": we treat it as if it were something we own, something we can admire and be fond of, in the same way another can admire and be fond of a picture or a piece of furniture we possess. We look at it. Not that we can see it very clearly, but we have the impression that, as we are on our knees, there is something very beautiful inside us that may be watched and observed.

Then this thing inside us has moods. Sometimes it is all tender and soft, sometimes arid; and we think that "My Spiritual Life" (in capitals) is now in a state of consolation, God showering His graces upon it, and now in a state of aridity, God providing the "bread of the strong."

But our spiritual life is not something objective inside us, as, let us say, our appendix, which may even be taken out without any loss. It is our very selves. We are praying, not some queer creature inside us. Moreover, if we are really praying, we are in contact with God all the time, whether we feel anything or not, whether distractions flit through our imagination or not. It does not matter at all whether our prayer is like this or like that. The one and only thing that matters is that we will with all our heart to give this time to God and that we are trying to give Him all we can, thinking about Him (not about ourselves), loving Him, and thanking Him for what He has done for us. But what "state" we are in, what our reactions are, matters not at all.

But, it may be objected, how can self-observation during prayer be something to be avoided, seeing that such a great saint as Teresa of Avila was in the habit of practicing it and even wrote books on all the details of her progress and her extraordinary experiences?

To this objection, the best, if somewhat impolite, answer is the old Latin proverb: *Quod licet Jovi non licet bovi* ("What is permitted to Jupiter is not permitted to the ox"). The present pages are written, not for spiritual geniuses, but for beginners in the life of prayer — led in the "ordinary" ways of this life, by which we mean without such special graces as visions, locutions, and the like. The less we consider ourselves exceptional beings with an extraordinary spiritual life, the better it will be for us, for the humbler and simpler we shall be; and it is these virtues that make us pleasing to God, not states of prayer.

If we seem to harp on this subject particularly, we do so because there seems to be for many of us a special danger to give ourselves the place in our prayer that should be occupied by God. This danger seems to be but a transposition into the spiritual sphere of the prevalent tendency of modern thought in the psychological sphere. It is, in an even larger context, part of the strange upheaval of values all around us. Not the objective law, but the subjective reaction, is the constant preoccupation of our contemporaries — whether we consider such phenomena as the advocacy of euthanasia or divorce (even by dignitaries of Christian communions outside the Catholic Church) or the refusal to recognize crime and punish it as such, because there is no longer an absolute right or wrong but only psychological adjustments or maladjustments. It is, therefore, not surprising that the tendency of the soul to be preoccupied with herself rather than with God — although known at all times — should be a particular danger of our own day. Therefore, we should take every precaution to avoid it as far as possible. Once we are conscious that this is a danger, rather than flatter ourselves that we are enjoying a very interesting spiritual life, the first step is taken to overcome it.

After this initial realization, what else can be done to overcome this tendency to self-observation? First, we must humbly ask God to help us to overcome this temptation. Second, we should resolutely turn away from the thought of ourselves and

our own prayer as soon as we become aware that we are thinking of these. We can do this most effectively by directing our
attention deliberately to one or other of those mysteries that
attract us most, be it the Passion, or the Blessed Sacrament,
the Divine Childhood or our Lady. Even if our thoughts
should stray again and again to ourselves, if we turn away every
time we notice it, the time of our prayer will have been well
spent.

And let us not be afraid to turn to those mysteries that give
us even an emotional satisfaction. There are some of us who
have read so much about detachment and the "Night of the
Senses" that they are terrified as soon as sensible images enter
their prayer, preferring to have wonderful thoughts about the
Blessed Trinity rather than occupy themselves humbly with
our Lord's humanity. Let us listen to the great St. Teresa, who
criticizes certain books giving such advice: "These books advise us earnestly to put aside all corporeal imagination and to
approach the contemplation of the Divinity . . . but I cannot
bear the idea that we must withdraw ourselves entirely from
Christ and treat that Divine Body of His as though it were on a
level with our miseries. . . . I can see clearly . . . that it is God's
will, if we are to please Him and He is to grant us great favors,
that this should be done through His most sacred humanity. . . .
He will show us the way; we must look at His life — that is our
best pattern."[108]

As soon, then, as we realize that, instead of praying or med-
itating, we are thinking about our spiritual life and watching

[108]*Complete Works*, I, 136-139.

ourselves, let us concentrate on a subject apt to arouse and quicken our love for our Lord, even if this kind of prayer should be somewhat emotional. It is better to be emotional about our Lord than to be inquisitive about ourselves. For the whole object of the life of prayer is to oust our ego from the center of our interest and to place Christ within this center, so that, one day, we may be able to say with St. Paul, "I live, no longer I, but Christ in me."[109]

There is another danger afflicting beginners, and even those who have made some progress in the life of prayer — a danger closely related to the one we have just been treating. It is the temptation to discuss our prayer with others. More often than not, our self-love disguises itself as humility and the desire to learn: we consult people, both priests and laymen, on methods and difficulties and so find ample opportunity for talking about ourselves and our own spiritual life. "My prayer . . . my contemplation [oh, this much-abused word!] . . . my spiritual life . . ." All the time, we hope that our partner will think us very spiritual and well advanced on the way of perfection.

Now, the desire to talk about our prayer to anyone except our director is nearly always a temptation. And even to our director we should say only what is necessary. To talk to all and sundry about our spiritual life is just a kind of spiritual exhibitionism. When the saints wrote about these things, they almost always did so at a very advanced stage of their life and under obedience, and, more often than not, found it a burden.

[109]Cf. Gal. 2:20.

There are people who will come to an unknown priest and after two sentences say, "You see, Father, I am a contemplative. I have such and such problems in my life of prayer. . . ." and then be disappointed if no sympathy is forthcoming. If we have temptations in this direction — and they can sometimes be very strong and disguise themselves as a genuine need for advice — let us meditate a little on this verse from the Canticle: "A garden enclosed is my sister, my spouse."[110] Just as a young bride would not tell her friends about the intimacies of her married life, so the soul, the bride of God, should not easily divulge what passes between her and the Lord in prayer. Can we think of our Lady, the bride par excellence, talking about her interior life to her friends? No more should we give away the secrets of the King.

There is a kind of spiritual modesty that will prevent us from discussing our prayer with anyone except our confessor or director, or, in exceptional cases, with another person in whose judgments we have particular confidence. Normally, however, the best way of learning how to pray will be by praying, not by talking about our prayer. And we shall best be taught how to do this by her whom God has appointed as our teacher — that is, by our Holy Mother, the Church.

[110]Cf. Cant. 4:12 (RSV = Song of Sol. 4:12).

⌒

Chapter Fourteen

Follow the Church's
liturgical year in your prayer

As we have been trying to show, if we approach God as our Father in all simplicity, we shall find prayer not at all complicated. Indeed, how could it be, seeing that we are exhorted to pray always? Perhaps the best rule is this: Pray as you can — and not as you can't. It is little use to read one book after another, to try one devotion after another, in order to pray as God wants us to pray.

As our Lord told us that He is the Way, prayerful thinking about His life will be a sure method of leading us to God. And the Church, our good Mother, gives us wonderful helps for prayer through the liturgical year.

⌒

Advent

In Advent, she asks us to reflect on the expectation of the whole world, and of our Lady in particular; she invites us to meditate on this new life that is growing in Mary of Nazareth, on the silence in which salvation is prepared for Adam's fallen race, on the perfect trust both of her and of St. Joseph. The chapters of Isaiah on the child that is given to us,[111] and the first chapters of St. Luke and St. Matthew will be the best food for meditation at this time.

☞

Christmas

Then, in Christmastide, our prayer will be all joyful. We can think to our heart's content about the goodness of God, who willed to be born poor, in a stable, welcomed not only by angels and wise men but by simple shepherds; so that He might be one of us, of all of us, whether we are poor simple folk or wise people or rich, bringing Him the gifts we have — whether it be only our prayer and devotion, special talents, or riches given to Him in His poor.

☞

Lent

After the last outburst of Christmas joy at Candlemas,[112] there comes the stern time of Lent, when we are bidden to reflect more earnestly on our own sins and the sins of the world; on our Lord's temptations and fasting in the desert, on the need for penance, for fasting, praying, and almsgiving.

Passiontide and Holy Week almost draw us into prayer without much cooperation from us: the Liturgy, the appearance of the Church wearing her purple veil of mourning, the

[111]Cf. Isa. 7, 9.
[112]That is, the feast of the Presentation of Christ.

last burst of joyful bells on Holy Thursday and the flower-decked altar of repose followed by the black absence of all joy on Good Friday: these will make us live the Passion in our prayer almost naturally, we might say.

⌒

Easter

And then the joyous Eastertide with the constant *Alleluia* will take our minds as easily into the risen life of our Lord, the Christ who died once but can die no more, and who, through Baptism and the Eucharist, has already given us a share in His risen life here on earth. The empty tomb, death and suffering already overcome, although still present with us: this will make the glory of our prayer in Eastertide, leading to the Ascension and to the outpouring of the Holy Spirit.

Sometimes, however, souls experience a special difficulty in adjusting their prayer to the Paschal season. Holy Thursday and Good Friday were so full of intensely human emotions that the risen Christ of the forty days[113] seems almost remote. Contact with the Crucified was so intimate, and now we have suddenly to deal no longer with a suffering body like our own, but with a risen one, impassible, passing through locked doors, saying, "Touch me not."[114] We are at a loss as to how to attune our poor human prayer to this season of superhuman glory.

But there is another side to this picture of the risen Lord. We need only think of His first appearance to Mary Magdalene,

[113]Cf. Acts 1:3.
[114]Cf. John 20:17.

of the infinitely tender exchange of those two words: *Mary, Rabboni.*[115] Or of that other scene recorded by St. John, when the Lord, after making the disciples take the miraculous draught of fish, set hot coals for them, all ready with fish and bread, so that they may have their breakfast after the night's labor.[116] It is as if, after the piercing sorrow caused them by His Passion and by their own humiliating part in it, He was now going to console them by pouring upon them His divine tenderness, as a mother would take her crying child into her arms and feed him and make him happy again by sheer gentleness.

Therefore, in our Paschal prayer, we should cast ourselves into the arms of our Lord like children, ready to be consoled for the hardships of Lent and the desolation of Good Friday. For the very marks on His body, which He so willingly showed to St. Thomas,[117] and which now plead in eternity before His heavenly Father for our sins, assure us that He is not now remote from us, but nearer than ever, the Divine Friend whose friendship can never fail.

☞

Pentecost

And so, when He ascends to Heaven after the great forty days, He does not leave us orphans. Between the Ascension and Pentecost, the Church enters a nine-day retreat, in company with our Lady and the Apostles, to await the coming of

[115]John 20:16.
[116]John 21:1-14.
[117]John 20:24-29.

the promised Paraclete. In these days, the Church in her Liturgy breaks out into a veritable paean of jubilation, as if she could not contain her impatience for this promised wonderful gift. And if we would really lead a spiritual life, we have to enter very specially into this spirit of preparation for the Holy Spirit. He is the supreme director of our spiritual life; from Him come all the gifts we need for our prayer.

The difficulty so many souls have in their relationship with the Holy Spirit is that they cannot apprehend Him with their imagination. Relationship with the Second Person of the Blessed Trinity is easy, because of the Incarnation. The First Person can be seized, however inadequately, through the human concept of Fatherhood. But for the Third Person there are no such helps. In recent times, the view has been expressed, especially outside the Church, that the Holy Spirit is particularly accessible to our contemporaries because He is a force; that we, being accustomed to deal with electricity and atomic energy, will easily understand a God who is spiritual energy. But this is a dangerous proceeding, because it leaves out the most important factor: the Holy Spirit is not a force, but a Person.

If we get in touch with the Holy Spirit — and we are brought in touch with Him in Baptism, and in a very special way in Confirmation — we get in touch with a Person, and with a most consoling Person. For to Him is attributed preeminently the work of sanctification; and since, being God, He is omnipotent, He will make us saints, provided we do not place obstacles in His way.

Therefore, if we can possibly arrange it, a retreat, whether preached or private, before Pentecost, and devoted particularly to the mystery of the Third Person of the Trinity, will be a great help in our prayer life.

Nor should we have any difficulty in addressing ourselves to the Holy Spirit. The Church herself has given us a glorious hymn, each verse of which provides ample food for meditation. She puts us in touch with a Person. In the *Veni Sancte Spiritus*, the Spirit is called Father of the poor, Giver of gifts, Light of hearts, excellent Comforter, sweet Guest of the soul. The less we think of Him as a mysterious Being outside us and the more we realize that this wonderful Person who is all love — for is He not essentially the love between the Father and the Son? — is within us, dwelling in our soul, the more easily shall we make conscious contact with Him.

We should often pray to the Holy Spirit, asking Him to teach us; for He is *the* teacher of Christians, of whom our Lord has said that He would guide us into all truth.[118] Therefore, the more eagerly we prepare for Him and the more ardently we desire His coming, the more efficaciously will the Holy Spirit renew His coming into our hearts at Pentecost.

☙

Holy Trinity

A week after Pentecost, the first half of the Church's year closes with the feast of the Most Holy Trinity. After Easter and Pentecost, this comes almost as an anticlimax; and it is true that the custom of keeping the octave day of Pentecost as the feast of the Trinity was introduced only comparatively late

[118]John 16:13.

into the Christian calendar. This is perhaps due to the fact
that the revelation of the Holy Trinity is not connected with
one definite historical event, as was the coming of the Holy
Spirit. Rather, it pervades the whole of Revelation, from the
Creation of the world to the Incarnation, and from the Incarnation to the foundation of the Church in the Upper Room in
Jerusalem; so we might almost say that every Christian feast is
a feast of the Trinity, because every feast is a feast of God and
God is the Trinity. We do not have a special "Feast of God."
Yet it was supremely fitting that, after celebrating the feast of
the Holy Spirit, the Church should desire to proclaim her faith
in the one God in three Persons by a special feast, thus com-
pleting her circle that began on the First Sunday of Advent.

The life of the soul follows in striking manner this pattern
of the Church's year; for, although the Holy Trinity pervades
the whole spiritual life from its beginning, it normally does not
become predominant until the last stages. St. John of the
Cross gives as the characteristic of the Transforming Union or
Mystical Marriage (that is to say, of the highest stage a soul can
reach in this life) that "the communication of the Father and
of the Son and of the Holy Spirit in the soul are made together, and are the light and fire of love in it."[119]

Therefore, it is often the case that in the beginning of the
spiritual life, the soul is more attracted to the humanity of our
Lord than to the August mystery of the three Divine Persons
in the one divine nature. This, of course, is as it should be. Yet
it will probably be a great help to many souls desiring a life of

---

[119]*Complete Works,* "The Living Flame," III, 206.

perfection, to dwell from time to time on the glorious privilege of having the three Divine Persons living in them. This is not a pious metaphor, but a tremendous reality. Our Lord said, "If anyone love me, he will keep my word. And my Father will love him, and we will come and make our abode with him."[120] Except for Truth itself, we could hardly have believed that this promise would be actually true. But, as we have His word for it, we are allowed to rejoice in this incredible happiness that, in the words of St. Thomas Aquinas, "by sanctifying grace the entire Trinity is the guest of our souls."

Reading the life and the collections of letters and sayings of the holy Carmelite Elizabeth of the Trinity[121] may help us to gain a deeper appreciation of this inestimable privilege. Then Trinity Sunday will become truly the feast of the God living within us, penetrating us to the depths of our being, while taking us out of ourselves and all the little pettinesses of our life, drawing us into His own eternal life, even enlarging and perfecting our souls, which were made in His image.

May, the month of Mary

Perhaps the best way of preparing both for the coming of the Holy Spirit and for the feast of the Most Holy Trinity is to do so in the company of Mary, as the Apostles did in the

[120]John 14:23.
[121]Bl. Elizabeth of the Trinity (1880-1906), Discalced Carmelite nun particularly devoted to the presence of the Blessed Trinity in her soul.

Cenacle. This is especially easy, as Pentecost and Trinity Sunday are celebrated either during or immediately after May, the month of Mary.

It may be that, despite all our efforts, we cannot find the right approach to these mysteries. Well, then, Mary, the Bride of the Spirit, will surely find a way for us. Some people — especially, of course, those brought up in Protestantism; but others also, notably the more highbrow Catholics — are almost afraid to give our Lady any but the very lowest place in their life of prayer, as if what is given to her were taken away from our Lord. If we do that, we need not be surprised that our spiritual life goes wrong and we cannot find the right way to pray.

A young Protestant woman once asked was it not wrong, if she had little time to give to prayer anyway, to "waste," so to speak, so much time on praying to our Lady when she could pray directly to God?

Now, the answer to this is that, first, no prayer to our Lady is "wasted time," because it is prayer through her to God. She occupies her exalted place in Heaven and in the Church of God for no other reason than that she is the Virgin Mother of God, most intimately linked with the Divinity through the fact that the Eternal Word took flesh from her. All her privileges, from her Immaculate Conception to her bodily Assumption into Heaven, derive from this. Therefore, if we pray to her, we are at once put in touch with our Lord — as, when she came to visit Elizabeth, St. John in his mother's womb immediately rejoiced in the presence of his Lord.[122]

[122]Luke 1:44.

But it is not only the *time* we give to praying to our Lady. In fact, comparatively little depends on that. Devotion to our Lady is a kind of spiritual consciousness — as a child is conscious of the love of his mother even without actually talking to her or consciously thinking of her. We know Mary is there, always ready to help her children; we turn to her in need, come and show our love to her, saying the *Angelus* or the *Salve Regina*. And through this devotion to our Mother, our life of prayer is somehow made simpler, more tender, and difficulties are smoothed out more easily.

With some people, it is almost a kind of pride that will not allow our Lady entrance into their life of prayer. "She is only a creature, after all, and prayer is direct relationship with God." But, as we have seen before, relationship with God means relationship with Jesus; and, if we accept Jesus, we have to accept His Mother, too. If we invite her into our life of prayer together with her Son, it will be not to our detriment. When we find ourselves poor, with all the wine of our fine thoughts and considerations spent, it will be she who will ask her Son, as she once did at Cana, to change the water of our aridity into the wine of contemplation.[123]

In the month of Mary, then, as we are preparing for the coming of the Spirit, let us make a large place in our spiritual life for Mary; for it is through her, as St. Louis de Montfort[124]

---

[123]Cf. John 2:1-11.

[124]St. Louis de Montfort (1673-1716), secular priest who founded the Sisters of the Divine Wisdom and the Missionary Priests of Mary and is known for his book *True Devotion to Mary*.

teaches, that by the action of the Holy Spirit, Jesus will be formed in us. And that is the goal of all prayer.

֍

Corpus Christi

On the month of Mary there follows June, which is dedicated in a special way to our Lord. The great liturgical cycle which began with the First Sunday of Advent closed with Trinity Sunday, which marks the end of Paschaltide. In the second half of her year, the Church is no longer concerned to follow closely the events of our Lord's life, but goes out into her vast inheritance, choosing among the mysteries those she desires to place before the faithful in a special way. It is only fitting that the first great feast after Trinity Sunday should be Corpus Christi.

How could we speak about prayer without mentioning the Blessed Sacrament, the food of our spiritual life, which causes our love to blossom forth into perfect charity and our prayer to develop into union with God? Our Lord, whose delight it is to be with the children of men, instituted the Eucharist on Holy Thursday so that He might remain with us in the most intimate union possible — as our very food.

Corpus Christi is the feast of thanksgiving for this most wonderful gift, and surely it is no mere coincidence that the greatest theologian of the Church, St. Thomas Aquinas, should have been chosen to compose the office for it. There are few poems of the Church in which theological accuracy and tender depth of devotion have been so perfectly blended as in the *Pange Lingua* and *Verbum supernum*, St. Thomas's hymns for

Vespers and Lauds of Corpus Christi, and the sequence *Lauda Sion*.

In the Blessed Sacrament, our Lord is so near to us and His love is so overwhelming that devotion may sometimes become overemotional. The idea of the "Prisoner in the Tabernacle," for example, which was condemned by the Church; and certain expressions, found even in approved spiritual writers — as if our Lord could still suffer in His eucharistic body, at least from our ingratitude — tend to nourish a not altogether wholesome piety.

Our Lord is as impassible in His sacrament as He is in His glorified body in Heaven. Else how could He be our food? The primary reason He gave us the Eucharist is to be our food, not an object of our worship. *"Cibum turbae duodenae se dat suis minibus"* ("By His own hands He gives Himself as food to the Twelve"), sings St. Thomas, and again in the Lauds hymn: *"Quibus sub bina specie Carnem dedit et sanguinem Ut duplicis substantiae Totum cibaret hominem"* ("To whom He gave His flesh and blood in twofold species that He might nourish the whole man of twofold substance").

Let us, then, rejoice on this glorious feast of our Lord, exposed in the monstrance, but even more in His sacramental Presence within us, so that we, too, may become a monstrance, as it were, showing Him forth to others. Without devotion to the Blessed Sacrament and as frequent Communion as possible, our spiritual life will remain cold and barren. The Eucharist is the very heart of our spiritual life, because it is a real union — although often unfelt — with His humanity and divinity.

☞

The Sacred Heart of Jesus

After Corpus Christi has been celebrated, our prayer will turn in gratitude to the love of Jesus that has given us this sacrament. For the feast of the Sacred Heart is nothing else but the feast of His love represented under the sign of the heart, the seat of love.

There are some people who find devotion to the Sacred Heart difficult — as if in it we were just worshiping a part of our Lord's body. Now, first of all, as the humanity of Jesus is hypostatically united to His divinity, there is no part of His body that we may not worship. Indeed, if we really believe Him to be God and man, we shall have the ardent desire to worship His body, which He turned into the instrument of our salvation by allowing His hands and feet and side to be pierced. It was the loving meditation on the wounds of our Lord, so widespread in the Middle Ages, that led to the discovery, so to speak, of His Heart. Whoever meditated devoutly on the wound in His side could hardly fail to arrive at the Heart that was pierced when this wound was made. This meditation, combined with the Gospel narrative of the Beloved Disciple resting His head on the breast of Jesus at the Last Supper, led to the rise of devotion to the Sacred Heart.[125]

It is true that most of the Sacred Heart statues and pictures are atrocious. But what has that to do with the divine Love streaming from this Heart? How can we fail to see that, in showing us His Heart, our Lord is inviting us to pray to Him

[125]Cf. John 13:23-25.

with absolute confidence, to cast all our sorrows, all our difficulties on Him? "Come to me, all you that labor and are burdened, and I will refresh you."[126] The more simply we approach Him through His love for us, the more surely shall we attain to that spiritual relationship with Him which is the content of all Christian prayer. For we have a right to this relationship; not, of course, through our own merits, which are nothing and are of value only because of our union with Him, but we have a right to it because we are redeemed by His Blood.

~

Feasts of our Lady

After this, the Church gives us a number of our Lady's feasts: Our Lady of Mount Carmel; then, of course, her greatest feast, her Assumption into Heaven; and, not too long after, her Nativity and her Seven Sorrows. How can we fail to forget our heavenly Mother when we are perpetually reminded of her by our earthly Mother, the Church? The Queen of Contemplatives, the Queen of Heaven, the Mother of Sorrows — all her mysteries are set before us, to make us ever more loving and confident and encourage us to entrust to her the prayer we offer God and her Son.

~

All Saints

Hitherto we have said little of the place of the saints in our life of prayer. The feast of All Saints is the fitting occasion for

[126]Matt. 11:28.

a few words on this subject. Of course, there are many more saints than those officially canonized by the Church. On the feast of All Saints we venerate these as well.

Now, the saints play a twofold part in our life: they are an example for us by their virtues, and they help us by their intercession in Heaven. Happily, hagiography in our time has changed its character; it is no longer, as it was in the past, an edifying enumeration of superhuman acts of virtue, especially of penance and of extraordinary graces and miracles. Most modern writers make every effort to enter into the psychology of the saints and to trace their development, their trials, their difficulties, and their victories over those human weaknesses that they share with all of us.

It is the greatest mistake we can make to picture the saints as gentle, milk-and-water characters, virtuous from infancy, with no more than a few trifling imperfections to overcome. The truth is almost the exact opposite. For the kingdom is of the violent,[127] and sanctity presupposes great strength of character; but the stronger one's character, the more difficult it is for fallen human nature to overcome itself and to practice the fundamental Christian virtues, such as humility and meekness, which go so very much "against the grain."

Who would easily believe that the "gentle" St. Francis de Sales was by nature a very violent character, given to outbursts of temper, which it cost him greatly to master? St. Thérèse of Lisieux, so severely detached, suffered as a child from excessive sensitivity. Her great, holy Mother, Teresa of Avila, was

[127]Cf. Luke 16:16.

not without strong temptations to vanity in her youth and liked lighthearted conversations in the parlor when she was a young nun. St. Francis of Assisi, St. Ignatius of Loyola, St. Margaret of Cortona,[128] and many others had felt — and sometimes succumbed to — all the temptations of the world and the flesh before they resolved to serve henceforth only one Master. Are we to believe that this resolve was made without a struggle? Or that grace suddenly obliterated all traces of their past life? Surely not. The Lord is not wont to make it so easy. "But," said St. Augustine, "if they, why not I?"

Let us make this the keynote of our prayer on the feast of All Saints. If we really love God, all things, as St. Paul says, will work together for our good.[129] All things — even, or, rather, especially, our faults. For our faults are our opportunities. If I am given to outbursts of temper, that is surely an indication that God wants me to reach sanctity by overcoming this propensity. If I am given to thinking the worst rather than the best of my neighbor, the practice of fraternal charity is meant to become my outstanding virtue. If I like food and drink more than is compatible with the spiritual life, a mortified taste is what God wants of me.

---

[128]St. Francis of Assisi (1182-1226), founder of the Franciscan Order; St. Ignatius of Loyola (1491-1556), founder of the Society of Jesus; St. Margaret of Cortona (d. 1297), mother who repented of an illicit relationship with a young nobleman when he died suddenly, became a Franciscan tertiary, received visions, and was the instrument of marvelous healings.

[129]Rom. 8:28.

All these faults are there, not to be feebly lamented as obstacles to holiness, but to be resolutely tackled and changed into so many virtues. If the saints succeeded, why should we not succeed? It is a theological principle that to him who does what he can, God will not deny grace. If we are determined to do all we can, God will give us grace so that we shall be able to carry out our purpose.

The saints, who have had the same struggles as we have while they were on earth, will help us not only by their example but also through their intercession. They see our needs far better than we do ourselves, because they see them in God; and they are ready to help us, because they belong to the same family as we, for we are members of the same Church: they of the Church Triumphant, we of the Church Militant.

From the very beginnings of Christianity, this sense of the oneness of the Church has been evident. How could it be otherwise, seeing that we believe in the one Church, united in charity in all her members, whether living on earth or in Heaven?

And as we believe that the life in the next world will be an immeasurably fuller, not a diminished life, our prayers in Heaven will be much more efficacious than our prayers on earth; our very charity will urge us to concern ourselves with the needs of souls on earth, which will be made known to us in the light of the Beatific Vision. Prayer to the saints will strengthen our consciousness of this bond of unity between all believers, which is so necessary for a full spiritual life.

It is an unchristian conception of mysticism to think of mystical prayer only as communion of the alone with the

Alone. The first commandment goes never without the second. The saint in the desert (and who would not think in this connection of the holy Fr. de Foucauld?) goes to God, who is not the Alone, but the perfect community of the Trinity, accompanied by a host of souls — in fact, by the whole Church. What other sense has the High Priestly Prayer of our Lord: "That they all may be one, as Thou, Father, in me, and I in Thee; that they may be one in us,"[130] if not that there is a supernatural unity in grace among all believers, modeled on the perfect unity of the Blessed Trinity Itself?

It is this unity alone that can overcome the false unity of the mass movements of our time, as well as the barren secular individualism that began in the religious individualism of the Protestant reformers. The feast of All Saints should remind us of it and engraft this truth profoundly in our prayer. For the more deeply we are conscious of the unity of the Mystical Body, the less shall we be in danger of succumbing to that unhealthy preoccupation with ourselves which, as we have seen before, is the great temptation besetting those who practice mental prayer. Just as "none of us liveth to himself,"[131] so none of us prays for himself alone. We pray in union, in communion, with the whole Christ, with our Head in Heaven and His Blessed Mother and all the saints, as well as with all our brethren on earth.

The more deeply living the communion with the saints in Heaven becomes to us, the more efficaciously will our prayer

[130] John 17:21.
[131] Rom. 14:7.

overcome all the dissensions and petty individualisms among ourselves and in the world.

⌒

All Souls

And this communion does not extend only to the saints glorified in Heaven, who can help us. The Christian life is a constant give and take; as we receive grace through those who have gone before us, so we can also obtain it for those who have not yet reached the blessed goal of the Beatific Vision.

As soon as the Church has concluded the feast of All Saints, the month of the Holy Souls has begun.

We need only look at ourselves in truth, at all our pettiness, self-love, lack of charity, to realize that (although our conscience may not blame us for having mortally offended God) if we were to die now, we would be in no way fitted for the awe-inspiring purity of the Beatific Vision. Yet, at the moment, we are so much occupied with all sorts of worldly concerns and distractions that this Vision of the Trinity seems to be something far away. We cannot say we do not desire it; but its attainment occupies us much less than the attainment of a livelihood, of a house, of a desirable marriage and similar purely earthly concerns. Yet, once this life is over, none of its cares will be of any significance, and the whole of our consciousness will be riveted to one thing only: to the attainment of that same Beatific Vision which has played such a small part in our earthly existence.

We know how profoundly we can suffer from the absence of a loved being, even though we may be as sure as we can be of anything on this earth that we shall see him again after a certain time. How infinitely greater will be the suffering caused by the absence of the one Being on whose enjoyment our eternal happiness depends, a suffering completely unalleviated by any distractions, but, on the contrary, enhanced by a certain felt punishment due to all those faults for which we did not make adequate atonement on earth. The souls who are now undergoing this suffering were very much like us when they were on earth; we can well understand all their shortcomings and infidelities, because we behave exactly the same. Shall we not have compassion on them and, as a merciful dispensation of Providence has given us the power, do all we can to relieve their sufferings by our prayers and by gaining indulgences for them?

Our Mother, the Church, gives us such wonderful opportunities of gaining indulgences, especially during this month of November. In doing so, we are fulfilling our Lord's commandment: "All things, therefore, whatsoever you would that men should do to you, do you also to them."[132] The charity of the saints toward us, our charity toward each other and toward the holy souls unites us with the whole Church, triumphant, militant, and suffering, in the one bond of charity, which is the bond of perfection.[133]

☞

Christ the King

The last Sunday of the Church year is dedicated to Christ the King, to whom we have also dared to dedicate this little

---

[132]Matt. 7:12.
[133]Cf. Col. 3:14.

book. The Church sums up what our Lord should mean to us in our earthly life in the feast of Christ the King. It is a "modern" feast, instituted by Pope Pius XI in 1925, and it meets a modern need. Ever since the "Reformation," there has been a growing tendency to divorce "religion" from "life," even in the Catholic world, despite the constant teaching of the Church to the contrary. And indeed it requires almost heroic virtue to swim constantly against the stream, to follow consistently the exalted principles of Christian morality while all the world around us worships material success. But if we truly believe Christ to be King, *the King,* from whom all earthly kingship derives its authority, then our *whole* life must be subjected to His will. This is a very difficult task and can be accomplished only by prayer.

Therefore, the feast of Christ the King should be an incentive for us to integrate our prayer more fully into our life and our life into our prayer. How is this to be done? Quite simply by bringing everything into our prayer. If we are preoccupied with some everyday problem, some difficult human relationship, some conflict of duties in our job, even a financial worry — let us take it into our prayer and ask Christ the King to help us resolve it in accordance with His will.

There is another way in which this feast should help us to deepen and enrich our spiritual life. It is only too easy to become more and more engrossed in our personal preoccupations without regarding the wider needs and interests of the Church. The feast of Christ the King should help us bypass this danger. There is no better means to forget ourselves than to think of the great concerns of the Church, ever anxious to extend Christ's rule over souls, rejoicing in her missionary conquests, profoundly grieved at the persecution of so many of her children, ever defending the truth and combating error. These things we should often make an object of our prayer, as did many great saints.

Chapter Fifteen

⌒

Center your spiritual life on the Mass

The Mass is the center of the Christian life, the meeting point of Heaven and earth. Those who desire to be truly spiritual will spare no effort to be able to attend it; and not only that, but to attend it in such a way as to draw the greatest possible graces from it.

Let us assume for a moment that Mass was said only once a year and only in one place. Would we not think it a most glorious privilege to be able to attend it, to have our Lord really present with us during that time, to be with Him on Calvary, and to participate in the torrents of grace that flow from the Sacrifice that the divine Redeemer has left to His Church? Surely we would spare no effort to go to this place once a year, as the Israelites spared no effort to go to Jerusalem on the Day of Atonement, however much we would have to sacrifice for the pilgrimage.

Or, to leave the realm of imagination and take an example from the bitter realities of recent times: what risks have priests and laymen taken in concentration camps; to what lengths of sacrifice have they gone, to be able to say or to attend Mass just once? We have it almost on our doorstep, and we prefer to turn over in bed, because a few minutes of sleep are more precious to us than our Lord is. Because, in His wonderful goodness, He has made it so easy for us to be with Him, we despise this very goodness and apply even to Him the proverb that familiarity breeds contempt. Is this, perhaps, one of the reasons why the Lord allows the persecutions of our time, so that we may once more learn to value the privileges He has showered on us, that we may again find it worthwhile to make some little sacrifice to meet Him on Calvary?

To be present at Mass as we ought to be, we must be there in faith. So many of us go to Mass wondering whether it will be Fr. X — "He takes so long to say Mass"; or Fr. Y — "He gabbles it so"; or perhaps Fr. Z — "He says it beautifully." It is but natural, for we see the priest, and we cannot see our Lord. Yet He who really offers the Mass is always our Lord, and it is He whom we should endeavor to see; not, of course, with our imagination — that could lead only to illusion — but in the light of Faith. We should always be conscious that what is taking place at the altar is the Sacrifice of Calvary; that our Lord offers Himself for us as He once offered Himself on Golgotha; that we really and truly assist at His Passion, at the sacramental outpouring of His Blood for our salvation. If we have once grasped this fully, not only shall we find it much easier to sacrifice our sleep and other little comforts for the Holy Mass, but we shall also be able to follow it more easily.

Knowing that the Divine Victim is actually present on the altar, our prayer will become even more intense, more personal; together with the priest, we will ask the Lord to accept this Sacrifice graciously. The Sacrifice is, indeed, always pleasing to God; it is we, the offerers, who desire to be changed thereby, so that we, too, may have a share with all the saints in Heaven. But a foretaste of the joy of Heaven may already be ours here on earth.

Our desire for Holy Communion will grow; with the priest we shall say the Our Father: "Thy will be done; give us this day our daily bread, our earthly bread, but also our heavenly Bread, which we shall soon receive."

As we have placed our needs before the heavenly Father, we become more and more conscious of the one thing we really need: love — love of God and love of our neighbor.

Are there still obstacles to the full blossoming forth of this love? There is One to take them away: "Lamb of God, who takes away the sins of the world, have mercy on us." We cannot do it, but He surely will. And so we go up to the altar.

Can we ever be worthy to receive Holy Communion, the most intimate union with the Body and Blood of Christ, with His divinity and His manhood? Of course not; but He, in His mercy, makes us worthy. By giving us grace, he has put on us the wedding garment, so that we may boldly come to His table to receive the supreme gift of His love, which is Love itself and, as St. Thomas teaches us, produces an increase of actual charity in the soul. The more often, therefore, we come to receive Him, the more we shall grow in charity, unless we ourselves place obstacles in its way by our unfaithfulness to grace.

How are we to use these precious moments after Holy Communion, when our Lord is actually bodily present within us? Some souls find it difficult to make a thanksgiving. They read the appropriate prayers from their missal or prayer book and find that they mean nothing; they have received Love itself and feel as dry and cold as if they had received nothing.

There is, of course, no necessity to feel anything, and a Holy Communion made in dryness may often be as pleasing to God as one made with fervor that we can feel — or even more so. Yet, surely this should not be the norm. Most saints have felt intense joy, peace, and contentment after Holy Communion except in periods of complete aridity; and even in those, it sometimes happens that the only rays of light are given after Holy Communion. Of course, if the Lord withholds this favor, it would be the worst possible procedure to try to work ourselves up into a state of emotion in which we might imagine we feel all sorts of things. This could only lead to illusion and unwholesome sentimentalism. What we ought to do is ask ourselves if we have not brought this dryness on ourselves through our own fault. If we willfully indulge in distractions during Mass, such as looking around to see who is in church, watching other people's behavior, and similar things, it is not surprising that our Lord would not want to make His Presence felt. This will be even more the case if we have strong attachments to creatures, which, although not actually sinful, prevent us from giving ourselves fully to God.

This, obviously, does not refer to normal, legitimate attachments. Love between husband and wife, between parents and children, or between friends will not prevent the enjoyment of our Lord's coming. Did not He Himself love His Mother, St. John, St. Peter, St. Mary Magdalene, and Martha and Lazarus with a full human love?

It is only when such an affection becomes possessive, when it fills all our thoughts and gets out of proportion, desiring its own satisfaction even at the expense of charity and justice, that it will become an obstacle, coming between us and our Lord. Yet, fallen human nature being what it is, such is the case more frequently than we imagine. A love, a friendship, seemed so innocent, so evidently willed by God, and, before we know how it happened, we are ensnared in an all-too-human affection, worrying and wondering, fretting and doubting, no longer realizing that God, the Lord of all things, will also take care of our human relationships.

If, therefore, we find ourselves cold at Holy Communion, we may well examine ourselves in this direction and, if we are conscious of an undue attachment, ask God persistently to help us rid ourselves of it. But if our conscience is clear in this matter, our difficulties may sometimes be due to a certain lack of freedom and spontaneity in our approach to our Lord in the Blessed Sacrament. He comes to us as a Lover; let us meet Him as a Lover. We do not read to a Lover from a book in order to tell Him that we love Him, nor do we use fine phrases and clever metaphors. "I love You" is generally quite enough; and sometimes there is no need even for that.

When our Lord is within us after Holy Communion, let us put down our missals or rosaries and recollect ourselves in His Presence, telling Him of our love for Him or remaining silent, for He knows all we want to say without our telling Him. Let us just "be with Him," as we are with a person we love, happy in one another's presence, secure in one another's affection. Let us not be formal in those precious moments; let us abandon ourselves to Love, who wants nothing more than to take possession of us. And if we find this impossible — well, our Lord told us Himself, "Ask and it shall be given unto you." So let us ask Him persistently to give us the grace to receive Him as lovingly as He desires to be received. This is a prayer that will certainly be answered.

It is a remarkable thing about the Mass that, after Communion, it is brought to an almost sudden end. We have hardly received our Lord, and we already hear, *"Ite, Missa est"* ("Go, the Mass is ended"). Why this abrupt conclusion after the long preparation? The reason is not far to seek. It is the Church's duty to instruct her children, to offer the Sacrifice, and by her prayers to place the soul in the right frame of mind to receive the Lord. But once Holy Communion has been given, our Lord Himself is with us; He will now take over, as it were. The Church leaves it to Him to converse with His own as He wishes.

Mass is quickly brought to an end. But this does not mean that we are expected to leave the church as soon as possible and to make a dash for the breakfast table. Now, with the Divine Word Himself within us, is the time to pray, to linger in His Presence, if possible — that is to say, if our daily duties do not prevent us from doing so. The great Friend and Lover is within us; shall we turn our back on Him immediately to occupy ourselves with other things?

If we can do so, we should stay on a little while, enjoying His Presence, thanking Him, loving Him; for it is in our hearts that He desires to dwell; it is for this purpose that He comes down to us at Mass and that He stays with us in the tabernacle.

His Presence there is a great consolation and certainly helps our prayer. But His Presence in our hearts is a far greater consolation; and the more we realize the infinite love that impelled Him to change bread, this humblest substance, into His Body in order to be united to us in the most intimate way possible, the more precious will be for us this time after Holy Communion, when He is so entirely, so palpably ours.

But let us make no mistake. Having devout feelings after Holy Communion is not a test of our love for our Lord. The true proof of it will be given during the day. We may sometimes have been continually harassed by temptations and distractions; and yet we may have made an excellent thanksgiving in the eyes of our Lord, although we ourselves may not know it. If we go back to our daily work strengthened, pacified; if we show our neighbor a smiling face; if we are ready to help, to forgive, to make sacrifices for others all day long — then, whatever our feelings may have been, our Communion will have borne rich fruit. If, however, we do none of these things, if we show no love, no patience with others, then, however devout we may have imagined ourselves to be, we shall have made no return to our Lord for His great love.

The outcome of our Lord's Sacrifice is to communicate Himself to us; the outcome of our communion with Him must be the sacrifice of ourselves we make to others and, through them, to Him. "In this we have known the charity of God, because he hath laid down his life for us; and we ought to lay down our lives for the brethren. He that hath the substance of this world and shall see his brother in need and shall shut up his bowels from him: how doth the charity of God abide in him? My little children, let us not love in word nor in tongue, but in deed and in truth."[134]

This is the *alpha* and the *omega*, the beginning and the end: love of God, expressed in love of the brethren. Let us come to Him and receive the sacrament of His love, and let us again go out from Him and bring this love to the brethren. This is the law of the Christian life; and if we keep this law of love, then, as St. Augustine says, we may do what we will: we shall always be pleasing to the one God, who is the Father, and the Son, and the Holy Spirit.

[134] 1 John 3:16-18.

~

Chapter Sixteen

Practice penance prudently

Penance is a very unpopular subject these days, even among Catholics. One of the main preoccupations of the world around us is comfort. "Be more comfortable" is the gist of most advertisements: more comfortable through tastier food, softer beds, faster planes and cars. The very idea that a person could bear discomfort with equanimity — except, of course, in wartime or in the pursuit of sports records — let alone actually seek it, is quite incomprehensible to most of our contemporaries.

Yet when our Lord walked upon earth, He said, "Deny yourselves . . . take upon you your cross. . . . Pray and fast, lest you enter into temptation."[135] And after St. Paul — who buffeted his body, lest, preaching to others, he should himself be found wanting[136] — there has not been one saint in the Church of God who has not done penance in one form or another.

In one form or another: we would stress that. Times change, and with them the general tenor of life. Places, climates, all

[135]Cf. Matt. 16:24; 26:41.
[136]1 Cor. 9:27.

sorts of other circumstances differ, and the forms our penances take will differ accordingly. Today we find spending our lives atop a pillar just as impossible as scourging ourselves nightly, the way St. Dominic and other holy people in the Middle Ages did — even laymen; or as impossible as walling ourselves up in a cell, the way certain medieval anchorites did. Even spending a whole Lent with only bread and water as our daily food, a penance recorded in the lives of many saints, will be impossible to nearly all of us, at least in many countries where the very climate would seem to forbid it.

Is this a matter for regret? We do not think so. Great physical "feats" of penance are in no way necessary to holiness and can sometimes lead to undesirable consequences in a kind of endurance test and even pride in our penitential exploits. In the realm of penance, as in every other department of the spiritual life, it is the intention that counts. The poor widow in the Gospel was recommended because, throwing two mites into the box, she gave all she had.[137] If we do the little penances our health and circumstances allow us for the love of God, we will be much more pleasing to Him than if we undertake violent austerities to gratify our taste for the extraordinary.

Let us make no mistake: very often it is precisely the small, inconspicuous penances that cost most. High up in the hierarchy of sanctifying penances are those of the tongue. Of course, we ought always to abstain from uncharitable talk, for that is sinful, and hence abstaining from it cannot be regarded as a penance. But to abstain from much talking if we are inclined

[137]Mark 12:41-44.

to it can be a very difficult penance. For even among very devout persons, there are those for whom keeping silence is a great trial. As soon as we are together with a friend, we just bubble over. Without restraint, we talk about our own affairs and those of others, assuming with selfish naïveté that what is of interest to us must necessarily be of interest to everyone else. For those of us, then, who are given to much talking, it will be an excellent penance to restrain our volubility and to give others a chance to voice their opinions.

If this is a good penitential practice for talkative people, the naturally silent ones can also find an opportunity for mortifying themselves, but in the opposite direction. They can sometimes become a real trial to others because they act as a damper on every conversation. For them it will be very salutary to overcome their natural disinclination and to contribute their share to their friends' entertainment, even if they find it difficult. The world is not a Trappist monastery. We are in charity bound to converse with our fellowmen, to listen to their views, as well as to express our own, to show them our sympathy, and to give them advice and comfort when they need it.

The "penances of the tongue" are varied and can be used to mortify many of our faults. To suppress, for example, a witty remark that would have produced much appreciation from our friends is very penitential for our vanity. Not to make a sharp repartee when attacked will mortify our self-love, and to refrain from a criticism can sometimes be a veritable act of charity.

But what about those penances that are strictly physical? They, too, can be very effective. If our health does not allow us to fast, we can mortify our sense of taste in innumerable little ways: we can pass over a particularly appetizing dish or forego salting or sweetening our food as much as we would like; we can dispense with a second cup of coffee; we can eat sweets only rarely. All these are significant little mortifications, yet, if practiced constantly, they can very effectively fulfill their purpose: to detach us from created things in order to draw us closer to God.

No spiritual life is balanced without the element of penance, but penance itself must be kept in sane proportion. We know the terrifying maxims of St. John of the Cross: "Strive always to choose, not that which is easiest, but that which is most difficult; not that which is most delectable, but that which is most unpleasing . . . not that which is restful, but that which is wearisome," etc.; and the principle of acting "against the grain."[138]

Are we to put these maxims into practice to the letter? To give a few examples: if we feel in need of a holiday, ought we to go on working? If the bright summer sun invites us to go for a walk or for a swim, ought we to stay at home and do some work that is not necessary? If we desire to pour out our heart to a friend, ought we to refrain from that, suffering silently in isolation?

If we were to act consistently on this principle, we would soon find ourselves on the way, not to sanctity, but to a nervous breakdown. The conditions of life in the modern world are such that a certain amount of relaxation is absolutely necessary. It is one thing to live the life of an enclosed monk or

[138]*Complete Works*, "Ascent of Mount Carmel," I, 61.

nun with few responsibilities and quite another to have to work in the world with a responsibility to a family or even only to ourselves.

We usually find ample opportunity for acting against the grain in our daily life without having to go out of our way to look for it. There is the daily toil of earning our living, the eight hours in the office, backbiting colleagues, exacting or irritable bosses, monotonous or uncongenial work, dreary surroundings, constantly ringing telephones, and financial difficulties. With all these we have to contend, having to act against the grain whether we want to or not. If we offer all this to our Lord in the same spirit as a religious offers his voluntary penances and the mortifications of community life, we shall find our means of sanctification ready-made. But in order to stand these conditions, we have to accept our relaxations, our holidays and innocent amusements happily and simply as the means to enable us to endure the strain of our daily life.

Let us listen to what St. Teresa, that sanest of saints, has to say on this point: "There are some people who think that devotion will slip away from them if they relax a little. . . . Yet there are many circumstances in which . . . it is permissible for us to take some recreation, in order that we may be the stronger when we return to prayer. In everything we need discretion."[139] If this was written to nuns, how much more necessary is this kind of discretion in the world!

In order to be able to give God what He wants, we have to relieve the strain of our daily life from time to time. To make a

[139]*Complete Works*, I, 74.

constant practice of always choosing the more difficult and wearisome thing, to act against the grain all the time would eventually make us incapable of carrying out the will of God at all.

In this, as in all other matters of the spiritual life, it is surely best to follow the example of our Lord Himself. When He and His disciples were hard pressed by the crowds, He did not tell them to act against their natural desire for repose, but said to them, "Come apart into a desert place, and rest a little."[140] He who had made man knew that constant strain is impossible to bear, except in some very special cases of apostolic work, when a particular grace is given to enable the body to carry on despite its powers' being overtaxed. In the same spirit of moderation, St. Paul advised St. Timothy: "Do not still drink water, but use a little wine for thy stomach's sake."[141]

In these things, it is essential and cannot be stressed sufficiently that the right balance should always be kept. The element of penance is very necessary in our lives. But on the other hand, we are spirits within a body; and if we have to earn our daily bread by the labor of our hands or brains, if we have to look after our household and our family, we have to guard against overstrain, for, if we break down, it will mean great difficulties for those dependent on us.

In this respect, we cannot imitate the examples of those holy monks and nuns we read about, who did penance without taking any account of their health. In a community, the

[140]Mark 6:31.
[141]1 Tim. 5:23.

necessary provision is made for nursing the sick, although, even there, superiors are usually careful to regulate the penances of their subjects in accordance with the rules of prudence. For men and women living in the world, this prudence is even more necessary, as long illnesses generally mean great distress for their families. If God sends them, we have to accept them gladly as His will for us and ours; but we have no right to provoke them by straining ourselves to the breaking point in our effort to lead penitential lives.

As we have seen in the beginning, common sense is a very necessary quality for those desiring to live a spiritual life in the world; and it has to be exercised particularly where there is a question of doing penance. If we are generous, if we really want to give God all He wants of us, we need have no fear to relax penance if "brother ass"[142] demands it imperiously. For penance is only a means, not an end in itself. It is necessary, but it should be used moderately; sufficiently to overcome our self-indulgence and spur on our love of God, but not so indiscreetly as to incapacitate us for fulfilling our duties. Combined with the loving acceptance of all those involuntary penances, great and small, which God sends us day by day, this voluntary mortification will stimulate and help our life of prayer and hasten our union with God, which is the end of all prayer and penance.

[142]St. Francis of Assisi's nickname for his body.

Chapter Seventeen

⁀

Accept the trials God sends to perfect you

From what has hitherto been said, it might seem as if the spiritual life were a succession of happy experiences, effortless meditation, and generously accepted penances. If we give ourselves wholeheartedly to God, we shall often find that during the first weeks or months of our newly discovered fervor, this will indeed be so. But we may be sure that, sooner or later, difficulties will arise. We shall suddenly find ourselves unable to meditate as we had done before; God will seem far away; our spiritual life will appear as something unreal.

Now, there may be several causes for this state. It may, for example, be due to indisposition, nervous strain, and the like. In this case, it will be advisable to ease our spiritual program, get more sleep or food, and generally give the body whatever the doctor deems necessary. Such relaxation will evidently be the will of God for us at the moment; shorter prayers and less frequent visits to the Church will be what He wants of us, and the generous acceptance of our ill health will amply compensate for the curtailing of our devotions.

More frequently, however, our sudden lack of "taste" for the spiritual life will be a normal psychological development. We have thrown ourselves with great vigor into this life, which opened up to us new vistas and new adventures; and suddenly there happens what so often happens in the natural life: we have a reaction.

To take an example from another sphere: those of us who have studied languages, mathematics, or any other subject to which we felt attracted know that generally, after the first period of delight and quick success, there will follow a time when we feel bored and are tempted to give up. We seem to be making no progress at all; the rules we thought we had already mastered now seem full of exceptions and pitfalls; the new book we are given after our elementary primer seems quite incomprehensible; in fact, we are convinced that we had better give up altogether because we are sure that the subject is beyond us. We have reached a deadlock.

But any experienced teacher will tell us that this is a perfectly natural thing; that we have actually made very satisfactory progress, although we may not realize it ourselves; and that it would be folly to give up at this stage. The thing to do is to go on plodding for some time, and after a few weeks or months, all will have become easy again and even more interesting than before.

Now, this is very much what happens in the spiritual life. For the life of the soul, besides, of course, being dominated in a very special way by grace, is also subject to the ordinary psychological laws. Thus, after some time, we shall probably find ourselves in a rather disagreeable state of languor — *acedia* — when we shall find nothing but boredom in our prayers and begin to wonder what it is all about. Would it not be much better to content ourselves with our ordinary duties as Catholics and give up all aspirations to a deeper spiritual life?

It would be folly, indeed, to give in to these temptations. Do we give up the work by which we earn our living because it is sometimes boring? Or do we imagine that monks and nuns never find their life monotonous? In fact, the previously mentioned *acedia* was a special monastic complaint, which used to assail even the most devout from time to time with suggestions to leave their vocation for a more "useful" or pleasant life in the world. And so we, too, are bound to have this experience, feeling that prayer time, which has become so dull and full of distractions, would be spent far better in some other, more "profitable" activity.

What are we to do in such a situation? The same as we would do if we had reached a deadlock in any other matter: go on, despite weariness and disgust, being confident that after this time of darkness, we shall once more emerge into the light.

There is, however, not only a natural, psychological side to these difficult periods, but also a supernatural one. When we are praying happily, full of delight in God and divine things, we may imagine ourselves well on the way to sanctity. Virtue and prayer seem to come so easily, and, without realizing it, we shall probably be very satisfied with ourselves. Thus, there will be a good deal of selfishness in our prayer. But when this is suddenly followed by a period of boredom and dryness, our prayer will no longer give us any satisfaction — quite the contrary.

And then will be the time when God will teach us to pray, not for *our* satisfaction, but for *His*. For even though we may feel that our prayer is quite useless, that all these thousand and one silly thoughts that come into our mind (which we are trying in vain to suppress) cannot possibly be pleasing to Him, God will not look at these distractions, but at our goodwill, our desire to please Him, and this will be more precious to Him than all our devout feelings that so easily make us self-satisfied.

This is a great danger at all times, but especially at the beginning of our prayer life. One of the most profitable results of these periods of dryness, however, is that they will teach us humility. For when we are there on our knees, desperately battling against hosts of foolish ideas, feeling as if we did not love God at all and as if all devotion and virtue had completely forsaken us, then is the moment when we begin to realize our own weakness. Then are we made to understand that all our devotion, all those fine thoughts that came so easily, were the gift of God, not our own achievement, and that our Lord's words are literally true: "Without me, you can do nothing."[142]

What, therefore, ought we to do in these times? Precisely this: make our own helplessness and utter dependence on God our prayer. When all those distractions and temptations assail us, let us firmly stick to our times of prayer and make wholehearted acts of loving submission to the will of God as often as we can. Let us especially beware of the thought that such unfelt prayer, or, rather, the feeling that we are not praying at all, is a waste of time. It is not. For we are doing something

[142]John 15:5.

extremely profitable and pleasing to God all the time: over-coming our own will, fighting against our own ideas of how we wish to pray, and submitting to the will of God by praying as He wants us to pray at this particular moment, although we ourselves cannot see any sense in it.

In doing this, we are emptying our understanding and forc-ing our will to obey, and are thereby practicing the virtues of faith, hope, and obedience, confident because, although we ourselves cannot see any purpose in our prayer, we know that we are in the hands of God, who will surely know how to turn even this seemingly useless trial to our profit and to His glory.

There is, however, one point we would make for those who have read about the "Dark Night of the Soul" of St. John of the Cross and who might perhaps be tempted to think that what they are experiencing is a similar interesting "mystical state." They will begin to watch themselves carefully and compare their dryness with the descriptions given by mystical writers.

To guard against such vain musings, we have begun with the psychological explanation. As has been said in the begin-ning of this chapter, such periods of dryness are bound to come in everybody's spiritual life; and, more often than not, they are just the inevitable psychological reaction that God is wont to use for His own purpose of purifying the soul and teaching it to depend on Him alone. If we take it as such, we shall derive great profit from this state of aridity. If, however, we begin to wonder whether it may not be the famous Dark Night, we shall turn to our loss what was given us for our gain. Instead of realizing our own helplessness, we shall become interested in ourselves and our "state" — a danger with which we have already dealt in Chapter 13, so that, rather than becoming more God-centered than we had been before, this trial will make us ever more self-centered. For pride is at the root of all our ills, and our perverted nature can find food for it even in those things that were intended for our humiliation.

We can only reiterate what we have often said before: the sole remedy is to look steadfastly at God and, while this trial lasts, not to ask ourselves what it may be and why God has sent it, but simply to accept it as just another proof of the weakness of our human nature, telling God that we are ready to bear with it as long as He wills it to last. This is most essential, for unless we know how to deal with these periods, which are really the decisive periods of growth, we shall never make any progress in the spiritual life.

As soon as we feel, therefore, as if we cannot pray at all, we must remain on our knees, telling God that, although we are quite incapable of giving Him any thoughts or feelings, we will at least give Him the time. "Not my will, but Thy will" should be our chief prayer during these periods. We must accept the limitations of our human nature, which is so susceptible to all sorts of ups and downs. Let us give this acceptance to God. It is only in eternity that we shall pray unceasingly with the full participation of all our powers.

These acts of acceptance both of the boredom and of the distractions should prevent us as much as possible from reflecting on our state. Let us often say to God — and to ourselves! — that it does not matter in the least what stage we have reached in the spiritual life, whether we are in the Dark Night of St. John of the Cross or just in the throes of an ordinary psychological reaction. The main thing is that we accept it joyfully and offer it to God with complete abandonment to His holy will.

If we do this, we shall derive great peace from our prayer: all vain worrying and wondering will cease; we shall just rest in His will as tranquilly as a little child in his mother's arms. We should therefore make the most of these times of trial; for the more generously we accept them, the greater will be our progress and the nearer shall we draw to God.

≈

Chapter Eighteen

Live in the spirit of poverty, chastity, and obedience

The essence of the religious life is in the three vows of poverty, chastity, and obedience. Therefore, they must also belong to the essence of the Christian life in the world, if it is truly lived to the full. But how can they be realized?

It is significant that Canon Law should make provision for laypeople living in the world to take one of these three vows, and one only — whereas for the other two the Church does not legislate. This vow, which any unmarried layman or woman may take with the approval of the confessor, is the vow of chastity.

Several saints took this vow spontaneously when they were still quite small children who could not possibly know the technical meaning of the term. Yet they evidently knew its true significance. For the vow of chastity in the Christian sense does not simply mean abstaining from marriage and any physical acts that belong to the sphere of sex. This is only its negative side. Far more important is its positive content — namely, the full giving of ourselves to God so as to choose Him spiritually in a way resembling the choice of a husband or wife, expressing the desire to enter with Him into a particularly close relationship.

This, of course, does not mean that the vow of chastity is the only way of preparing for a close union with God. There are married saints, such as St. Thomas More[144] or Bl. Anna Maria Taigi, who reached perfect union with God without having to sacrifice the happiness of married life. In fact, one of the most crying needs of our time is for holy marriages: marriages from which will spring vocations to the priesthood and the religious life, as well as for saintly lives lived in the world. But these marriages, too, must be based on chastity — that is to say, in the spirit, not the letter, of the vow.

The whole trend of our age goes against chastity, especially chastity in married life. One glance at the number of divorces suffices to show this. What seems to be at the base of so many modern marriages is not the desire to face the difficulties as well as the enjoyments of life together, not the wish to build a home and raise a family, with the acceptance of all the sufferings and sacrifices that this may entail, but the desire for the fulfillment of physical passion and for "having a good time."

When a marriage is truly Christian — that is to say, if both man and woman will to give themselves to God and, in and through Him, to each other — then this marriage will be lived in the spirit of chastity and will bear the fruit that God desires.

It is the great fallacy of so much loose talk about physical relationships that people imagine that by giving full rein to

[144]St. Thomas More (1478-1535), Lord Chancellor of England and martyr.

physical passion, they will enrich their life, even the life of the soul. Yet ever since the Fall of Adam, physical instincts, although good in themselves, tend to drag man down unless they are strictly controlled by reason and will. It is their control, not their indulgence, that makes a full human life possible.

An important distinction, however, has to be made. Control of passion, whether in dedicated celibacy or in Christian marriage, does not mean prudishness, nor is it likely to lead to sour joylessness. A holy priest bears not the slightest resemblance to a dried-up bachelor, or a nun to an arid spinster. Quite the contrary. A true priest will have in the highest degree the tenderness as well as the firmness of a father, and a true nun will be the most maternal of women. How could it be otherwise, since the Lord Himself is their Spouse, giving them a host of spiritual children, brought forth by prayer and sacrifice?

The fullest human life is not the life of many lovers, but the life of the one Lover, *This Tremendous Lover*, as Fr. Boylan calls Him in his well-known book. Whether we keep ourselves for this Lover alone, as we do by the vow of chastity, or whether we receive a husband or wife from Him, as we do in a marriage lived in the spirit of the vow, we shall find that our whole human life, soul and body, will be enriched beyond compare.

As we have said at the beginning of this chapter, the vow of chastity, by which we consecrate ourselves entirely to God, may be taken by laypeople in accordance with the provisions made for it by Canon Law. The two other vows of religion, however — poverty and obedience — are not provided for in this way, although individual priests sometimes allow their penitents to take them. The omission of both these vows from Canon Law has its reason. The vow of chastity is made immediately to God, and there are hardly any difficulties about its interpretation. What it entails is clear, and, with the help of God, it can be kept without human advice; faults against it can be confessed and absolved in the ordinary way.

It is different with the vows of poverty and obedience.

For the religious, it is evident what poverty means: he has given up all rights to property by his profession, and his personal needs are met in accordance with the rule of his order and the decisions of his superiors. Things are entirely different in the case of a person living in the world. To begin with, he cannot give up all rights to own property of any sort. Or else how could he keep himself and his family? If he evidently cannot give up these rights, but should nevertheless vow to use his possessions according to holy poverty, how could it be ascertained in what exactly this poverty consists in each particular case? Moreover, where is the lawful authority to make such decisions (should this be possible), since neither the parish priest nor the individual confessor or director has such authority?

It would, therefore, seem much simpler to resolve, without formal vow or promise, to live in the spirit of poverty in accordance with our status in life. For just as, say, the Franciscan lay brother has a standard of poverty different from that of a General of the Jesuits, and the Poor Clare from a Benedictine Lady Abbess, so, only in a far more marked degree, will it be in the world. The director of an industrial corporation cannot live in the same way as his bookkeeper, nor the wife of a minister like a domestic servant. But they can all live in the same spirit of

Live in the spirit of poverty, chastity, and obedience

poverty, for this spirit is essentially the spirit of detachment from material things.

Although he may actually live in dire poverty, a man who constantly hankers after possessions cannot be said to be poor in spirit. In the same way, a man who owns much property, but uses it as a trust received from God in a spirit of detachment, cannot be said to be rich in the sense in which riches were condemned by our Lord.

If, then, we would live in the spirit of poverty, we must detach our hearts from our possessions, as well as from the desire for possessions. The difficulty is how to achieve this.

Of course, the first thing to do if a difficulty confronts us is to pray about it. Constant and fervent prayer for detachment from earthly goods is the first condition for living in the spirit of poverty. But prayer alone is not enough. Things are comparatively easy for those of us who are not particularly well off. Then our daily life will probably offer many tests of our love of poverty. If we really have the spirit of poverty, we shall cheerfully do without many things that we would like to have, instead of grumbling because they are beyond our reach. We shall not compare our indigence with the superfluity of others; or if we do, let it be only to praise God because He has given us fewer temptations to lose our heart to worldly possessions.

If, however, our circumstances allow us to live at ease and to gratify our material desires, it will be necessary to deny ourselves certain luxuries very frequently. Opportunities for such sacrifices will abound. We might deny ourselves some superfluous piece of furniture or clothing that we intended to buy and give the money to some poor person we know or to some charitable institution. We may give up expensive drinks and cigars or cigarettes, at least for a time — not to swell our bank account with the savings, but to give alms. All this, however, must be done as quietly and unobtrusively as possible, for we should always remember our Lord's command not to let our left hand know what our right hand does.[145]

The most difficult of the vows of religion to keep in the world is, of course, the vow of obedience. To this applies even more pertinently what has been said about the vow of poverty. Neither our parish priest nor our director is entitled to accept vowed obedience in the way a superior of a religious community has the right to the obedience of his subjects. Such a vow, moreover, would involve us in even more difficulties than a vow of poverty, since we could never find out with certainty what is a matter of obedience and what is not. Incidentally, it would present endless problems, not only to us, but to the priest to whom it was made. The case of St. Jane Frances de Chantal, mentioned before, is very much to this point: her director, in wanting to hold her to a vow that it had become impossible for her to keep, evidently overstepped the limits of his authority and thereby caused great suffering to her and all manner of inconvenience to St. Francis de Sales.

If, however, a formal vow of obedience is considered impracticable by many directors, its spirit is all the more necessary and can be exercised by all of us every day of our lives.

There is, first, the obedience of the Christian to God, represented on earth by the Vicar of Christ, our bishops, and

---

[145]Matt. 6:3.

Live in the spirit of poverty, chastity, and obedience

parish priests. We live in obedience to the doctrines and the moral precepts of the Church; and this means accepting them, not because they happen to be in accordance with our views, but because they are willed by God. Hence we shall always accept them, even though they may be irksome or even seem unreasonable to us, because we are blinded by passion or prejudice. We sometimes hear that people have fallen away from the Church "through no fault of their own" but just because their parish priest was an unpleasant type of person, rattled through his Mass, or neglected his duties to his parishioners.

No doubt such things happen. In fact, far worse ones have happened in past centuries and may happen even now in certain places. But they are emphatically no reason for leaving the Church. The Church herself is without spot or wrinkle, although individual members may be very sinful indeed. There was a Judas among our Lord's chosen disciples, and the Church has always been a Church of sinners as well as of saints.

The Mass remains the Mass, the Body of Christ His Body, whether the priest who offers it is irreverent in his bearing or not. Naturally, it will hurt us deeply to see the Holy Sacrifice offered in a manner we deem unworthy of it; but it is still the Sacrifice of our Lord. To refrain from going to Mass for such a reason is an insult to Him and a mortal sin. We have no right whatever to assume that God will forgive us because it is the priest's fault that we no longer came to Mass. It is not the priest's fault; it is ours, because, through some private resentment, we did not obey the commandment of the Church.

Obedience goes deeper than that. We should come to Mass, even to weekday Mass, not only because we like it, because it feeds our devotion, but because our Lord told us that unless we eat His Flesh and drink His Blood, we shall have no life in us.[146] This should prevent us from coming to Mass only when we feel like it and from staying away when we find it more convenient.

It is in the same spirit of obedience that we should accept the penances the priest gives us in Confession. They are normally just trifling, a few short prayers; but if we say them, not from routine and because it is so easy, but because we desire to obey the ordinance of God mediated through His priest, this act of submission will increase the value of our penance in the sight of God and bear much fruit in our whole spiritual life.

It is not only in these more strictly religious acts that we can practice the spirit of obedience. If we desire to be truly spiritual, obedience will enter into every act of our dally life. Whatever may happen to us, we shall receive and accept it all as the will of the Father, without grumbling, without bitterness. Such obedience may often be as crucifying as religious obedience in the technical sense — sometimes even more so. For it involves not only direct obedience to God, but, as in the case of the religious, the far more difficult obedience to creatures and to the circumstances of our life.

If we truly believe that our lives are guided by Divine Providence — and we must believe it, for our Lord Himself tells us so[147] — then we shall accept *all* things, even tyrannous and unjust employers, cantankerous colleagues, and unpleasant

---

[146]John 6:54 (RSV = John 6:53).
[147]Matt. 6:25-34.

landlords or tenants, as the will of God, in obedience and loving submission.

This, of course, does not mean that we should not seek to improve our lot, that we should not try to change our job, our dwelling, or any other unpleasant situation in which we may find ourselves. Christian trust in Divine Providence is not fatalism. We may employ both prayer and all legitimate activities to bring about a change. But as long as the trial lasts, we should accept it lovingly and, if we can, joyfully, as a precious opportunity of proving that our desire for obedience is real, that it is not just a pleasant religious daydream that is shattered at the first contact with hard reality.

This kind of obedience — accepting all the trials of life with conscious submission, regarding even the most unpleasant and uncongenial persons we have to live with, or tasks we have to carry out, as so many manifestations of God's will — is generally far more difficult than obedience to a director in a few matters regarding prayer and penance.

There are many very devout persons who will not stir a finger without permission from Father, yet who will grumble and worry at every little misfortune that may befall them. Yet God does not use only our director or confessor to make known His will to us; far more often, He will speak to us in the everyday circumstances of our life, in the big and little sacrifices that are demanded, in the acts of kindness for which we are given an opportunity, in the annoying behavior of others that we are asked to bear with cheerfulness — all of which God asks us to accept as so many acts of obedience, and which we only too often turn into acts of rebellion.

This obedience is very difficult to exercise, precisely because it must be practiced day by day, and because it strikes right at the roots of our self-will. In fact, it would be impossible to achieve it, if there were not Someone to help us, Someone who became obedient for our sakes, obedient unto death, even the death of the Cross.

If we could only realize what this obedience must have meant to Him, the almighty Son of God. Do we really understand the tremendous passage in St. Paul's letter to the Philippians, where he presents our Lord's example of obedience for our imitation? "For let this mind be in you, which was also in Christ Jesus," he writes: this mind of the God-Man, on which he asks us to model our own little minds, who "emptied Himself, taking the form of a servant, being made in the likeness of men, and in habit found as a man. He humbled Himself, becoming obedient unto death, even to the death of the Cross."[148] If we would only keep our minds fixed on Him, the God hanging on the Cross, despised and spat upon by His own creatures, who could not so much as exist one moment without His making them and keeping them in being; if we could only keep this marvel of obedience firmly ingrained in our consciousness as the living source of our own attitude of obedience, then our difficulties would soon vanish, and gradually those around us would be able to discern the image of Christ shaping in us.

For it cannot be repeated often enough: sanctity does not consist in long visits to church or in much spiritual reading;

[148] Phil. 2:5, 7-8.

not even in frequent confessions and daily Communions, although these are necessary for achieving it. We probably all know people who do all this and yet seem to be strangely lacking in true obedience to God, whose will, expressed in the circumstances of our daily life, they constantly disobey. But it is precisely in obedience that sanctity consists. "For whosoever shall do the will of my Father that is in Heaven, he is my brother, and sister, and mother."[149]

If we would truly live in the spirit of the vows, let us live in chastity, in detachment from material things, and, most difficult of all, in detachment from our own will. It is hard; it is difficult; but we shall find our reward not only in Heaven but here on earth; for the reward that will be given to those who love and obey Him with all their heart is the "peace of God, which surpasseth all understanding."[150]

[149]Matt. 12:50.
[150]Phil. 4:7.

Chapter Nineteen

Live your Faith
even in the world

In the preceding pages, we have endeavored to show how it is possible to lead a truly spiritual life in the world. It is our conviction that far more souls are called to such a life than is commonly supposed. In fact, we believe that the only hope for our secularized, dechristianized society lies in being leavened by Christians living their Faith to the full in the very midst of this society.

This, however, is a difficult task. To swim constantly against the stream, to judge always by the standards of Christ rather than by the standards of mammon, to exalt poverty, chastity, and obedience rather than wealth, sensuality, and power — such truly Christian warfare needs not only a rich measure of divine grace and a strong character, but also human help and encouragement. And it is to our priests that we shall naturally turn for these.

The history of the Church is happily full of the records of heroic priests who, by their perfectly supernatural lives, were an inspiration to their people and drew crowds of disciples and converts. We need only think of John Bosco,[151] and the Curé d'Ars.

What was it that gave these men such an extraordinary influence? They were all truly fathers of the people, ready, like the Good Shepherd, to sacrifice themselves for their flock at any moment. They knew the deep truth of our Lord's words that to give is more blessed than to receive; that the priest, the *alter Christus*, must be the giver, the dispenser not only of God's spiritual blessings in the sacraments, but also the giver of every comfort and assistance, especially in the life of the soul.

Of course, such a vocation demands a self-emptying that is formed on the self-emptying of Christ[152] — an emptying that is hard to human nature. For although the sacrament of Ordination gives great graces to the priest for the fulfillment of his high office, his human nature with all its faults and weaknesses remains the same; just as the human character of all of us remains the same, although the sacrament of Confirmation has conferred upon us all the gifts of the Holy Spirit in a particularly efficacious manner.

It is perhaps the greatest compliment that both Catholics and Protestants can pay to the priesthood that we all expect priests somehow to be saints. We do not mind much if the doctor is impatient with us or if the lawyer has more time for a rich client than for a poor one. But if a priest behaves in the same way, we are immediately tempted to think him unworthy of his calling.

---

[151] St. John Bosco (1815-1888), founder of the Salesian Order.
[152] Cf. Phil. 2:7.

But let us remember that the priest, too, needs the sacrament of Penance; that, unknown to us, he may be putting up a fierce fight against his faults. It is for God to judge him, not for us, who are only too ready to see the mote in a priest's eye instead of trying to extract the beam from our own.

Yet it must be admitted that a priest, by the very fact of his vocation of an *alter Christus*, another Christ, has a far greater responsibility than any layman; that it is therefore inevitable that a priest's behavior should be judged by a much higher standard than, say, that of a doctor or a lawyer. A priest may be as intelligent, as well-mannered, and as easy to get along with as possible. Still, his ultimate success as a priest will always depend on his personal holiness.

It is a remarkable phenomenon that the holier a priest is, the less concerned he is with flattering wealthy parishioners and the more devoted he is to the poor and the sick, the more money will pour in for his charities even from the purses of those rich people over whom he disdained to make a fuss, as one less holy might have done. For, as so many lives of the saints have shown, holiness attracts — attracts even money when needed.

But it attracts more precious things than money: it attracts souls. A holy priest will rarely have to upbraid his people for being late for Mass. His own love of God, his own enthusiasm, will be contagious, and the people will follow his example. Not at once, perhaps; but if they see him leading a holy, self-sacrificing life month after month, year after year, sooner or later, the hard shell of their indifference will be broken. It was by prayer and penance that the Curé d'Ars transformed his little village, where vice and indifference held sway, into a model parish and a place of pilgrimage.

Normally, a small group of souls longing for a deeper spiritual life will quite naturally gather around such a priest and look to him for guidance. For many of us feel dimly a call to greater effort, to more generous self-giving, yet we know not how to answer it. Too many of our priests, as also of us laymen and women, still make this division in our minds: here the religious life and perfection, there the world and, well, imperfection. We soothe our sometimes slightly disquiet conscience with the consideration that we decidedly have no religious vocation and that therefore no greater effort is required from us, beyond, of course, keeping out of mortal sin and going to Mass on Sundays and saying our prayers. We say to ourselves that we are neither monks nor nuns; we have to live and get on in the world. And very often we find priests only too eager to confirm us in this view; they are quite willing to encourage a religious vocation, but they give little help to a vocation to perfection in the world.

Yet help is urgently needed. The paganism around us can be countered only by a vigorous spiritual life, and for this, an intimate cooperation between clergy and laity is indispensable. Such cooperation will, of course, have to rest on perfect mutual confidence. The layman must be ready to receive from time to time even sharp rebukes and humiliation from the priest; but, on the other hand, the priest will also be ready to accept suggestions and even respectful criticism from laymen.

It is surely time to abandon the still widely held view that for a layman to spend a considerable amount of his time in prayer is both waste and presumption, because prayer is believed to be the prerogative of the "professional" contemplatives, whereas laymen should employ themselves much more "usefully" in all manner of worldly activities. The purpose of this book has been to combat this essentially modern prejudice. It is to our priests that we turn with the request to help us in this fight against the overactivism of our time, the demons of which surely are driven out, not by committee meetings (although these may sometimes be necessary), but above all by prayer and fasting.

We cannot fight the spiritual battle alone. We must have all the help that can be given by understanding and advice, by providing as full a liturgical life as is possible according to the circumstances of the parishes, and, more important than all else, by the example of priestly lives consumed by the love of the Master and of souls.

There is no mistaking the signs of the times. "Unless your justice abound more than that of the Scribes and Pharisees, you shall not enter the kingdom of Heaven."[153] The children of darkness are ready to sacrifice themselves, to give their time and energy to their sinister cause in a measure far exceeding us easygoing Christians, "for the children of this world are wiser in their generation than the children of light."[154] The Church, our Mother, needs us.

Stalin is reported to have once asked how many army divisions the Vatican has. We are the "divisions" of the Vatican,

[153]Matt. 5:20.
[154]Luke 16:8.

armed with the "armor of light" of which St. Paul speaks![155] And what is this armor? The apostle tells us clearly: "Stand, therefore, having your loins girt about with truth and having on the breastplate of justice; and your feet shod with the preparation of the gospel of peace. In all things taking the shield of faith, wherewith you may be able to extinguish all the fiery darts of the most wicked one. And take unto you the helmet of salvation and the sword of the Spirit (which is the word of God). By all prayer and supplication, praying at all times in the spirit; and in the same watching with all instance and supplication for all the saints."[156]

What, then, are to be our weapons against "the most wicked one"? The most spiritual possible: truth, justice, peace, faith, the word of God, prayer, and watching. These were the weapons of the Church by which, about sixteen hundred years ago, she conquered a supposedly invincible empire intent on destroying her. With these same weapons, we shall conquer the enemy of the Church in our time.

But we must use them. Let us show forth truth and justice in our lives; let us rely on the faith given to us by God against all the temptations besetting us; and let us pray, pray at all times "in the spirit," as the apostle tells us, "and in the same watching with all instance and supplication for all the saints." Let us examine our conscience as to whether we are sufficiently concerned with the needs of the "saints," with those suffering persecution, with those under terrible temptation to give in to

[155]Rom. 13:12.
[156]Eph. 6:14-18.

such as would separate them from the Church; let us pray that their judgment and loyalty may remain clear and firm, despite what may be truly termed "the wiles of the Devil" to confuse them and to make them yield to what may so easily appear to them as the lesser evil.

Unless our faith, our hope, and our love are strong and constantly fed by a life of prayer and penance, we shall be failing in our duty toward God and toward these "saints." The times are too serious, the struggle is too intense, for us to be content with just an "ordinary" Christian life — if, indeed, there is such a thing. Is it to be said to us, what the Spirit said to the Church of Laodicea: "Because thou art lukewarm and neither cold nor hot, I will begin to vomit thee out of my mouth"?[157] We have to make our choice.

We — both clergy and laity. For we are all responsible. We all have our share in the guilt of the world. We have disregarded our Lady's call for prayer and penance; we have been seeking our own rather than the things that are God's. Our own infidelities, our bickering, our jealousies and enmities, our lack of charity and submission to the will of God: all these are so many causes that have contributed to make the world what it is now.

Therefore, if we want to save this world, if we want to bring it back to God from the wilderness into which it has strayed, we have to begin with ourselves. As God is above space, so our spiritual life does not depend on space. The prayers and sacrifices we offer here can and will have their effect where they are

---

[157] Apoc. 3:16 (RSV = Rev. 3:16).

needed. But they must be offered in the humble spirit that acknowledges the guilt of us all.

Some little time ago, I happened to meet a priest unknown to me. We talked about the political situation, and I mentioned this poignant feeling of guilt we have of sharing the responsibility because of all our faults and shortcomings. He looked at me in amazement. "But we are not responsible," he exclaimed. "I do not want communism. I am responsible for all sorts of things, but not for that." I tried to make my meaning clear, pointed to the prophecies of Fatima. But he only shook his head: this was absurd; we were in no way responsible for the state of the world and, hence, could do nothing about it.

Such has never been the attitude of the saints. We remember how St. Catherine of Siena firmly believed that her sins (and what she called her sins we would hardly regard as infinitesimal imperfections) were responsible for the plight of the Church, how she offered herself again and again for the salvation of Rome and the Church. Unless we all, both clergy and laity, develop a profound sense of personal responsibility for the evils of our time, our spiritual life will be unreal. For we are spirits in a body, living in space and in time, brothers of *all* men because of our common descent from Adam, brothers more especially of all the members of the Mystical Body because of our Baptism. Each of us having sinned in Adam, we cannot disclaim all responsibility for the sins of mankind — especially since we have added innumerable personal sins and infidelities to that first sin. For, although Original Sin itself was removed by Baptism, its effects remain and make us prone to evil.

To disclaim all responsibility for the evils of our time is to act like the Scribes and Pharisees in the story of the woman taken in adultery. They would disclaim all responsibility for this particular sin. Our Lord thought otherwise. "He that is without sin among you, let him first cast a stone at her."[158]

We are sinners living in space and time. We are all involved in the common guilt of our kind. Let us frankly acknowledge it, and let us make amends for it, as Our Lady of Fatima asked us to do. We owe it to God; we owe it to our martyrs, the hecatombs of bishops, priests, religious, and laymen suffering and dying for the Faith. We owe it to ourselves, placed by Divine Providence in this age of materialism and atheism to battle with the forces of evil.

But how can we do battle if we are listless and indifferent because we feel that we are not responsible and cannot do anything anyway? "I can do all things in him who strengtheneth me," says St. Paul.[159] We have the Church, the sacraments. We have the whole Trinity dwelling in our souls by grace — and we say we are powerless, we can do nothing? We can do all things because if we have a living faith, it is God Himself who strengthens us.

We may not see the results of our lives of sacrifice and prayer; indeed, in most cases we shall see nothing at all. But that does not mean that there *are* no results. There were no visible results of the prayer and sacrifice to be seen during the life of St. Thérèse of Lisieux, which was spent for the greater

[158]John 8:7.
[159]Phil. 4:13.

part in aridity and darkness, unknown in its heroism even to most of her own sisters in religion. Yet what tremendous results had this unseen, entirely uneventful little life! What conversions has it effected, how many souls has it transformed, what immeasurable good has it done to the Church and to the world! A life that was nothing except prayer and sacrifice, the exact fulfillment of her duties of state, a few chapters of autobiography and a collection of letters and poems.

Faith, hope and charity, prayer and sacrifice: these are the weapons to be used in our battle with the evil around us and with the evil within us. Let us use them generously, lovingly, fighting the holy war against sin, indifference, and tepidity, both in ourselves and in others, in the service of Him who "is the Head of the body, the Church; who is the Beginning, the Firstborn from the dead, that in all things He may hold the primacy,"[160] Christ the King.

[160]Col. 1:18.

⮑

Hilda Graef

(1907-1970)

Ironically, Hilda Graef, the author of this commonsense approach to the Faith, was once a superstitious atheist! Indeed, she was once so irrational that she avoided entering Catholic churches for fear that if she did, she'd become a Catholic — even though she was convinced that there was no God. Soon, however, her superstition and her atheism gave way to the grace of God.

Graef was born in Germany and raised a nominal Protestant, but her parents were actually unbelievers. She had, by her own account, "more than one Jewish grandmother,"[161] but had little contact with Judaism as a child. Her own atheism was confirmed when a cousin, whom Graef called "the genius of the family,"[162] told her that the New Testament contained

---

[161]Walter Romig, *The Book of Catholic Authors*, 5th Ser. (Grosse Point, Michigan: Walter Romig and Company, 1943), 126.

[162]Ibid., 125.

only fairy tales. Nevertheless, interested in broadening her horizons, at age seventeen Graef attended May devotions at a Catholic church. Captivated by an inexplicable attraction, she returned two days later to attend a Sunday Mass. "That finished me," she said. "I felt sure that if I went once more into a Catholic church, I would want to become a Catholic — without even believing in God."[163] So she determined to avoid entering Catholic churches.

Despite Graef's unbelief, the Hound of Heaven persisted: even while she was an atheist, Graef's interest in religion continued. She studied Scripture at Berlin University. She hoped to become a fashion journalist and nearly got a job on the staff of *Vogue,* but instead followed her mother's advice for a less flashy but perhaps more stable career: she earned a teaching degree and became a teacher of English and Scripture at a Berlin church school.

When Hitler rose to power, however, Graef's Jewish background became a threat to her survival. She left her teaching job, stopped publishing articles (which she had been doing since her university days) and found work as a housekeeper. When she was finally able, she left Germany for Holland and, ultimately, England.

In England, Graef had trouble making ends meet. She worked as a maid until she found teaching work at what she described as "an incredible little private school near Eton, whose principal was addicted to the brandy bottle."[164] She began to

[163] Ibid.
[164] Ibid., 126.

write again, placing articles in Swiss newspapers. But she suffered from the cold in England, and worried that her English
would never be good enough to allow her to write for English
journals.

But the Hound of Heaven was still at work. After several
years in England, she was given an opportunity to study the
theology of the Church of England. Her theological essays
at King's College, London, earned high marks from her pro-
fessors and increased her confidence in her ability to write in
English.

Graef joined the Church of England, although she later
confessed that at this point she "was still not much of a Christian."[165] Yet all of that was soon to change: in the course of her
studies, she discovered the doctrinal teachings of the Church
in the first five centuries. She suddenly saw the Faith clearly as
a perfectly logical whole, "and by no means absurd."[166]

Her conversion to Catholicism was now in progress; it was
brought to completion through some unfortunate circumstances. Graef earned her degree in theology, but was unable
to find work. She had retained her German nationality, but
with the advent of World War II, Germans weren't getting
hired in England.

She was reduced to living in a London attic that she described as "frequently shaken by bombs,"[167] and to depending
on a small allowance from a charitable organization. Finding

[165]Ibid., 127.
[166]Ibid.
[167]Ibid.

herself with plenty of time on her hands, she began to read Catholic classics: St. Thomas Aquinas and St. John of the Cross, as well as modern writers such as G. K. Chesterton and Monsignor Robert Hugh Benson. She began making morning and evening meditations according to the method of St. Ignatius.

These holy writers' works again bore fruit: in January 1941 Graef finally went to a Catholic Church and asked for instruction, "to the accompaniment of the noise of roaring planes and anti-aircraft guns."[168] She was received into the Church soon afterward.

Graef wrote many articles for such publications as *Blackfriars, the London Tablet, Commonweal,* and *The Torch,* as well as a number of books, including *The Way of the Mystics,* biographies of the mystic Therese Neumann and of St. Edith Stein, and her own autobiography. She also did substantial work on the writings of the Greek Church Fathers.

Intellectually honest and spiritually questing, Hilda Graef had a keen ability to find God — and to lead others to find Him — not only in advanced states of prayer and profound doctrines, but also in the ordinary things of everyday life.

[168] Ibid.

⤳

Sophia Institute Press®

Sophia Institute™ is a nonprofit institution that seeks to restore man's knowledge of eternal truth, including man's knowledge of his own nature, his relation to other persons, and his relation to God. Sophia Institute Press® serves this end in numerous ways: it publishes translations of foreign works to make them accessible to English-speaking readers; it brings out-of-print books back into print; and it publishes important new books that fulfill the ideals of Sophia Institute™. These books afford readers a rich source of the enduring wisdom of mankind.

Sophia Institute Press® makes these high-quality books available to the general public by using advanced technology and by soliciting donations to subsidize its general publishing costs. Your generosity can help Sophia Institute Press® to provide the public with editions of works containing the enduring wisdom of the ages. Please send your tax-deductible contribution to the address below.

For your free catalog, call:
Toll-free: 1-800-888-9344

Sophia Institute Press® ✦ Box 5284 ✦ Manchester, NH 03108
ww.sophiainstitute.com

Sophia Institute™ is a tax-exempt institution as defined by the
Internal Revenue Code, Section 501(c)(3). Tax I.D. 22-2548708.